# INDUSTRIAL
# HYDRAULICS
# TROUBLESHOOTING

# INDUSTRIAL
# HYDRAULICS
# TROUBLESHOOTING

**James E. Anders, Sr.**

**McGRAW-HILL BOOK COMPANY**

New York   St. Louis   San Francisco   Auckland
Bogotá   Hamburg   Johannesburg   London
Madrid   Mexico   Montreal   New Delhi
Panama   Paris   São Paulo   Singapore
Sydney   Tokyo   Toronto

**Library of Congress Cataloging in Publication Data**

Anders, James E.
    Industrial hydraulics troubleshooting.

    Bibliography: p.
    Includes index.
    1. Fluid power technology.  2. Oil hydraulic
machinery—Maintenance and repair.  I. Title.
TJ843.A53   1983       621.2′028′8       82-21691
ISBN 0-07-001592-9

1234567890   BKP/BKP   89876543


ISBN 0-07-001592-9


*The editors for this book were Diane A. Heiberg and Virginia Fechtmann Blair,*
*the designer was Naomi Auerbach, and the production*
*supervisor was Teresa F. Leaden. It was set in Baskerville*
*by J.M. Post Graphics Corporation.*
*Printed and bound by The Book Press.*


*All photographs in this book were taken by the author.*

To my wife, Jessie McHaffie Anders

## About the Author

JAMES E. ANDERS, Sr., a fellow of the Electro-Hydraulic Society of America, is currently hydraulic engineer at a large eastern Pennsylvania steel plant. A mechanical engineering graduate of Lehigh University, he has over 30 years' engineering experience. In addition to troubleshooting thousands of hydraulic systems in the plant, he has been associated with all of the more than 100 new systems introduced into the plant since 1972. He has designed a half-dozen new systems himself, and redesigned many more. He also teaches basic industrial hydraulics, mobile hydraulics, and specific system hydraulics in courses and seminars inside and outside of the company.

# CONTENTS

Blank Machine History and Component Record History Cards
follow the Index.

# PREFACE

I wish to acknowledge the encouragement given me by Mr. Lawrence G. Shea, USN, Retired, to put my thoughts on paper. I also wish to acknowledge the efforts of Mr. Benjamin H. Pinckney and Mr. Michael Stilwell for their many suggestions and the proofreading and suggestions by my wife, Jessie McHaffie Anders.

I thank my friends in the hydraulic field who so graciously supplied the various hydraulic components for photographic purposes.

There are hundreds of circuit arrangements in use in hydraulics today. It is not possible to consider all of them in the limited space of this book, so only a few circuits and components which constitute those most frequently encountered in my troubleshooting experience are mentioned.

The descriptive data given cannot possibly be valid for all manufacturers' components, so referral to proprietary component literature is suggested for any variances.

# INTRODUCTION

The troubleshooting techniques presented in this book consist of procedures which have proved to be successful. They have proved to be timesaving and functional, although there are many other approaches available. After you have been involved in hydraulic system troubleshooting for a while, you may discover that a different approach works better for you, and you are urged to follow whatever approach works best for you.

As time goes by and you get involved in more and more troubleshooting experiences, you are bound to discover that past successes help immeasurably toward new success. The various information that you have gained in your work is a tremendous help in new jobs. If you are genuinely interested in improving your troubleshooting capability, keep a log on every job you go out on. Write down the fault as it existed when you arrived on the scene. Write down the sequence you followed in diagnosing the problem. Write down what the true fault was discovered to be. It will not be long before you will be saying to yourself, "I had that problem on so-and-so system, and the fault was such and such." When you walk to the area of the new problem, you will be forearmed for this new problem because you have had previous experience along that line. The more troubleshooting you do, the better you get at it. It is just like any sport or game—the more you practice, the better you get. Read all the literature on componentry that you can. The more you know about a particular component, the better are your chances of identifying it as a possible trouble source. This knowledge can also lead to your eliminating the particular component as a possible fault source.

# INDUSTRIAL
# HYDRAULICS
# TROUBLESHOOTING

# 1

# SAFETY—FIRST, LAST, AND ALWAYS

In order to be able to continue to do the best job of trouble-shooting, it is imperative that you keep safety foremost in your mind. A hydraulic system is like an accident waiting for a place to happen. It is impossible to note every potentiality, so assume in every instance that the system is under pressure, the accumulator is charged, and the actuator will always move in the wrong direction when you loosen the pipe joints. You must use common sense, plan the job in advance, and learn what the hazards of working on hydraulic systems can be.

A few essential safety items for successful hydraulic trouble-shooting are listed below.

**Explain the Job and Hazards.** If you have people working with you, regardless of their craft take the time to explain what you intend to do and how they will be affected by it. You must do this whether they are working for you or for some other supervisor. Explain the job hazards. Take the workers to the area and point out those parts which may be moving during your testing and troubleshooting period. Make certain that people working directly under your supervision understand that they must not take any action at any time without first getting clearance from you. The job may take a little longer, but everyone will go home after work uninjured.

**Post Warnings When Possible.**  On certain jobs it may be necessary to post signs in the immediate area warning of the potential motion of moving parts and telling people to keep out of the area if at all possible. If you can possibly do the job without assistance, get the operator out of the area to avoid actuating anything by accident. If you cannot post warning signs, personally check for clearance and safety of operations every time you expect to cause any actuator motion that could be hazardous.

**Secure the System before Disassembly.**  Before you do *any* disassembly, lock out the electrical power source, bleed the system, and make sure the pressure gauges read zero. A correctly designed system will have valves at the accumulator so that you can bleed the accumulator pressure. Be certain that you have adequately shored any overrunning loads on cylinders to prevent their motion when you take the lines apart. Operate the manual and electrical directional control valves by hand a few times to bleed any remaining pressure. Check the pressure gauges to be sure that they read zero.

**Assume There Is System Pressure.**  Before breaking into the system, even though you have carried out the above steps, assume that there is system pressure in all the lines and actuators and work accordingly. If you must loosen threaded pipe, tubing, or hose joints, loosen them only partially. Wait for the flow of fluid to slow to a mere trickle. When this leakage rate is down to a few drops, then and *only* then is it safe to complete disassembly. If you must remove pipe flanges or components from baseplates or manifolds, loosen those bolts which are farthest from you, but by only one turn. Loosen the bolts closest to you just enough to break the original installing torque. If no fluid flows at that time, loosen the original bolts another turn or two. This creates a wedge-shaped opening, with the wide side of the wedge facing away from you. Any fluid will flow toward this wide wedge if there is residual pressure in the component, and you will not be subjected to the force of the fluid. After any fluid flow slows to mere drops, it should be safe to complete the removal of the component.

**Provide a Bucket to Catch any Fluid.**    Each and every time that you find it necessary to enter a system for component removal, inspection, or bleeding of air from the system, make sure that you have a bucket large enough to catch the drippings. This removes the extreme hazard of slippery flooring and reduces any potential for fire if the fluids are flammable. It also aids in good housekeeping.

NOTE: Do not reuse the fluid unless you filter it through a 10-micron filter.

To end this section on safety, I feel that it is necessary to review the suggestions.

■ Avoid working on "hot" equipment when possible.

■ Treat every entry into the system as though the system were under normal working pressure.

■ Know the hazards and prepare accordingly.

The importance of being safety-conscious in hydraulic troubleshooting cannot be overemphasized.

# 2

# BASIC REQUIREMENTS

To successfully troubleshoot industrial hydraulic systems, you must consider many items. Although the material presented here is deliberately limited to industrial systems, it also applies in varying degree to troubleshooting mobile equipment and machine tools.

The troubleshooting approach to use depends on the age of the system. In a new system at the time of start-up, you cannot rely totally on existing schematics. Last-minute changes often occur too late to be included in the drawings. In old established systems, invariably, no one enters the hydraulics changes actually made in the system on the drawings.

To become successful, the troubleshooter must be aware of five things at all times.

**1. Standard Hydraulics Symbols.** The troubleshooter must have an intimate knowledge of the hydraulics symbols. You may run across symbols published by the American National Standards Institute, or ANSI (formerly the United States of America Standards, USASI, and the American Standards Association, ASA), the International Standards Organization, ISO, or various professional societies, depending on who made the drawing and when. Unfortunately, some of the symbols may also be "company standards" or personal preference symbols of the person who made the drawing.

2. **Component Configurations.** The troubleshooter must learn the outward appearance of the various components made by the various manufacturers and associate these components with the appropriate symbols. Because the average system has so many components, it is not sufficient to know only the symbol for the component. Troubleshooting must be done out in the field, which means you must be able to see the component and know what it is. Some systems are designed and installed with components from but one manufacturer. That is becoming the exception rather than the rule. Most systems in use today make use of the components of various manufacturers.

3. **Component Function.** The troubleshooter must know how, and preferably why, the various hydraulic components function. Knowing the how and why of the various hydraulic functions of the components in a system makes it possible on occasion to pinpoint faults that occur. In many instances it is possible to rule out a certain component as being the cause of a fault, and you can therefore concentrate on the other components in the system.

4. **Information Evaluation.** The troubleshooter must not accept information supplied by those who request the troubleshooting aid as totally accurate. If the people making "suggestions" could correct the fault, they need not have called a troubleshooter in the first place.

5. **Control Circuit Analysis.** The hydraulics troubleshooter must know the basics of electrical control circuitry and symbols and the operation of the various relays (time delay on energizing and on deenergizing, etc.) This knowledge is essential to troubleshoot the various solenoid-type valves. Often the troubleshooter has to tell the electricians where the potential problem lies when the problem is not really hydraulic. (See Section 8, Electrical Control Circuits and Servos.)

The first four skills are not too difficult to acquire. Proficiency in control-circuit analysis takes longer.

# 3
# TROUBLESHOOTING OLD SYSTEMS

Let us assume that you have the first four of the five basic requirements. If so, you are prepared to troubleshoot systems. Knowing the fifth, electric control circuitry, will help you when the electricians try to win the inevitable argument as to whether a fault is hydraulically or electrically oriented.

## BASIC PROCEDURE

Be prepared to follow four steps each time that you are called out to troubleshoot an old system.

**Study the Drawings.** Unless you have memorized the hydraulic line diagram of the system you will be working on, take the time to get the drawing out of the files and review it before you go to the jobsite. Familiarize yourself with the various cylinder and motor functions and components in each subcircuit of the drawing. A look at the electrical ladder diagram at this time helps also. When you get to the job, many people ask questions, generally hindering you. Having studied the drawings thoroughly allows you to establish your credibility.

**Take Drawings Along to Jobsite.** Take the drawings to the jobsite. If you have to trace lines to locate certain components, the drawings will help. If there are mechanical drawings available showing the various pipe routings and components, they should also be brought to the jobsite. Quite frequently, the hydraulic line diagram is inadequate because some of the componentry gets placed under, over, or behind the structures, and you therefore need the mechanical drawings.

**Ask the Operator.** Have the operator describe what seems to be wrong with the system. If there are many subcircuits in the system and only one is malfunctioning, you can concentrate on that subcircuit. If all subcircuits are malfunctioning, another area of concentration is required.

**Test the System.** Run the system yourself so that you can see the "apparent" malfunction. First make sure that you can safely operate it, and double-check this factor yourself. Observe what does or does not happen. By doing this you will not have to rely on other people's opinions, but you can pay particular attention to that area mentioned by the operator. You can determine whether the problem is generalized, such as one caused by pump failure, or is in a specific subcircuit. To qualify the two basic areas where hydraulic faults occur, I will refer to generalized faults and subcircuit faults. *Generalized* faults, those in the immediate area of the power package, include the reservoir, pump, motor, and pressure relief valve, all of which are in the immediate area of the reservoir. *Subcircuit faults,* those in all other areas except that of the reservoir, include the directional control valves, actuators, and other miscellaneous components.

To clarify this distinction, consider a multiactuator circuit. If one actuator seems to be malfunctioning and the rest of the actuators are working correctly, we have a subcircuit fault. If nothing works (as would be the case with a bad pump, which is in the area of the reservoir) we have a generalized fault.

## CASES IN TROUBLESHOOTING

The rest of this section consists of cases, or examples, in which you work with line diagrams of theoretical circuits and line diagrams of various components. Assume that certain faults have occurred and attempt to find the fault or faults by analyzing the drawings.

### Hydraulic Cylinder Subcircuit Fault (Manual Control Valve)

Figure 1 shows a typical hydraulic circuit using three cylinders, two solenoid-controlled directional control valves, and one manual valve, plus other appropriate components.

Let us assume that cylinders no. 1 and no. 3 are working correctly, and that there is no motion of cylinder no. 2, either up or down, when the manual valve is actuated to get cylinder rod motion. The problem itself tells us quite a bit. First of all, the pump, pressure relief valve, filters, drive motor, and fluid conduits are good. If not, all three cylinders would be nonoperating. This is proof that there is a subcircuit problem.

We can now concentrate our efforts on that one subcircuit. Figure 2 shows only those items in that subcircuit. The only component failures which could possibly cause nonoperation of cylinder no. 2 must be in this subcircuit.

This is a good place to insert "Anders' Troubleshooting Law No. 1." It is this: If there is a knob, dial, handle, switch, or appurtenance of any type which can be turned, twisted or rotated, it will be. Corollary No. 1 to that rule is: Nobody touched it.

There are only so many factors which influence the operation of this no. 2 cylinder. Remember Troubleshooting Law No. 1.

The fastest and generally best approach to use is one in which the easiest tests are made first and no disassembly of components is required. Try to follow the sequence in which disassembly tests are last.

Since we have decided that the fault is subcircuit in nature, it is appropriate that we look only at that section of the drawing to do our troubleshooting.

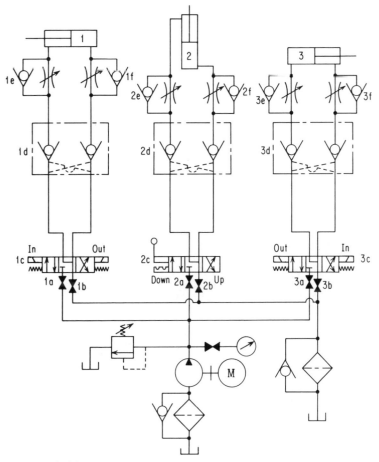

**Fig. 1**  Typical hydraulic circuit.

Figure 2 includes just those parts which could possibly affect the operation of the no. 2 cylinder. You must make certain that the load on the cylinder is not greater than the design load. You do not have to check the reservoir fluid level since the other two cylinders are functional.

The following seven steps are listed in a sequential manner so that disassembly is the last possibility mentioned.

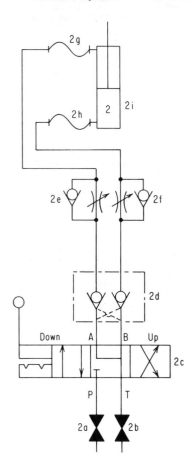

**Fig. 2** Detail of Figure 1 showing those parts of the circuit that affect no. 2 cylinder operation.

**Step 1: Check Isolation Valves.** Check the isolation valves (marked 2a and 2b) to make sure that they are fully open. If either one is fully closed, there can be no cylinder rod extension or retraction, since the fluid path would be closed completely. If they are both fully open, go on to step 2.

**Step 2: Check Control Valve Operation.** Manually operate the directional control valve (2c). Does it move correctly? If it does, you can temporarily rule it out as the cause of the problem. If you cannot move it, it could be the fault, but there are other possible causes as well. Let us, in this instance, say that the valve can be operated in any position, and therefore rule it out as the cause of the malfunction. Go to step 3.

**Step 3: Check the Flow Control Valves.** Determine whether the flow control valves are correctly adjusted (2e and 2f). Has someone been turning the dials? Mark the present position of one flow control valve. Rotate it fully clockwise, counting the number of turns. Divide the number of clockwise turns by 2, and now turn it counterclockwise by this amount. What you have done is turned the flow control valve to its midpoint, assuring some fluid flow if there are no internal problems in it. Adjust the other flow control valve by the same technique. This is the best approach to use to get flow through the valve for the next part of the test. Turn the system on and operate the directional control valve in both directions of operation. If the rod will move in one direction but not the other, you have found your problem to be a faulty flow control valve. You may also have found that someone has been maladjusting the flow control valve. Generally when one valve is malfunctioning, the conical part of the adjustable flow control valve has come free from the threaded portion and is acting like a check valve since there is nothing to keep it off its seat. Of course, this is not true for all types of adjustable flow control valves, so a look at the manufacturer's catalog may be necessary.

Let us suppose that the flow control valve adjustments have not changed the situation. The cylinder rod still does not move. It is safe to say that the flow control valves are good. We must look for the problem elsewhere.

**Step 4: Feel Cylinder Barrel.** If the cylinder's piston seals are leaking, it is possible to check for this leakage by feeling the cylinder barrel. The easiest way to do this is to place the directional control valve lever in either the rod-extend or rod-retract position, and leave it there. Now go to the cylinder location, being careful that you will not be in a pinch point, where the rod motion may catch you if it moves. Feel the entire cylinder barrel with your hands. If there is an internal leak, as may be caused by piston seal failure, there will be a hot spot in the area of the seal leak. Don't forget that horsepower equals gallons per minute times pressure in pounds per square inch, all divided by the constant 1714. Horsepower can also be expressed in British thermal units, which measure heat. When there is an internal leak, the fluid is moving from a high-pressure area to a low-pressure area at a given rate of flow dependent on the size of the leak. If there is no definable hot spot, you can be practically assured that the piston seals are good. Go on to step 5.

**Step 5: Increase System Pressure.**  Go back to the pump and reservoir area. Make certain that the pressure gauge shutoff valve is open, and have the system started up, with all directional valves in the neutral position. This will make all of the pump's output go across the pressure relief valve. Check the pressure gauge for the reading. Write this pressure in a book. To do the next step you must know the maximum point to which you may safely raise the system pressure. The parts and service catalog of the component manufacturer will tell you the pressure range. Slowly increase the system pressure to the maximum point. Operate the no. 2 cylinder directional control valve. If the lack of motion of the cylinder rod was due to mechanical binding (usually due to ambient dirt), the additional pressure operating on the no. 2 cylinder will in all probability be great enough to move the rod, in which case you have discovered the malfunction to have been caused by dirt in the ways. Don't forget Pascal's law that force equals pressure times area. For every square inch of piston area, the new higher pressure will create a new higher force on the rod's extension or retraction. If the piston rod now moves, you can be certain that it was the mechanical binding which prevented its original motion from occurring. Place the no. 2 cylinder's directional control valve lever back in the neutral position, and reset the pressure relief valve back to its original pressure setting. (You had recorded it in a book.) Clean up the cause of the binding. If this step has not solved the problem it is necessary to go on to step 6. Up until this point there was no need for piping disassembly.

**Step 6: Check for Flow Blockage.**  This step requires extreme caution, especially if there is a load on the cylinder rod. Shut the system down. Move the no. 2 cylinder's directional control valve from the UP to the DOWN position and back again a few times. This will relieve the line pressure.

Partially loosen the hose fitting closest to the no. 2 cylinder port (2g) catching any leaks in a container. When leakage ceases, remove the hose from the cylinder. Install that hose in a pipe tee (same pressure rating as the rest of the piping), which has a pressure gauge in it of the same rating as the main system pressure gauge. In the other side of the tee install a bar-stock valve of adequate strength for the system pressure involved. Close the bar-stock valve, and start up the system. Move the no. 2 directional control valve to the DOWN mode. This will send fluid through the valve, through the pilot-operated check valve, and through the flow control valve. The pressure gauge that you installed should read approximately the same as the main system pressure relief valve setting. If it does not read approximately the same, it means that there is a fault in the fluid conduit (pipe or hose), or the pilot-operated check valve for the down mode of operation is not good. The fault in the conduit could be caused by crushed conduit or, in the case of hose, the inner tube may have separated from the reinforcing material and be held closed by system pressure, much the same as a flapper-type valve is closed. Repositioning the gauge and bar-stock valve on the exit side of the flow control valve will show if the fault was a hose failure. The pressure gauge should show the appropriate pressure now, if the hose was at fault (approximating main system relief valve pressure setting). If no pressure is indicated at this point, the pilot-operated check valve must be the problem. With the system shut down, it is necessary to take the pilot-operated check valve apart to find the cause of the failure.

NOTE: Most failures in this valve are caused by particulate matter binding the pilot piston or plunger, preventing it from lifting the check poppet from its seat; this bound plunger thereby prevents reverse free flow of the fluid.

**Step 7: Check Cylinder Leakage.** Shut the system down. This last step requires extreme caution and is required only if all the other steps have not satisfied you. With the system turned off, connect the gauge and valve assembly to the (2h) cylinder port. Close the bar-stock valve. Place the no. 2 cylinder's directional control valve in the UP mode. Turn the system on. If the piston seals are leaking, the bar-stock valve is closed, and there is a load on the cylinder, a gauge reading should occur. The pressure reading would depend on the leak and the load. Now, hold the hose end over a container, and slowly open the bar-stock valve. If the piston seals are bad, the fluid will flow from the bar-stock valve with some velocity, since there is a flow path between the cap side of the cylinder and the rod side of the cylinder by means of the leaking seal. If this was the problem, replace the cylinder and readjust all valves to their original settings.

### Hydraulic Cylinder Subcircuit Fault (Electrical Control Valve)

Let us go back to Figure 1 again, only this time let us assume that cylinders no. 2 and no. 3 are functional. The only difference in approach to troubleshooting this situation is the difference in the directional control valve for the no. 1 cylinder and the no. 2 cylinder. The same basic approach to troubleshooting would be used as in the previous example, except we now have to deal with an electrically operated directional control valve rather than a manually operated one.

**Step 1: Check Isolation Valves.**  Check the isolation valves (1a and 1b on Figure 1) to make sure that they are fully open. If one or the other is fully closed, no fluid can flow, and the cylinder rod cannot extend or retract. Make certain that they are both open and go on to step 2.

**Step 2: Manually Override Control Valve.**  In the case of direct-acting solenoid-operated directional control valves, we still have the option to manually override the valve by means of the manual overrides available at each end of the solenoids. If manual override of the solenoid causes the cylinder to function correctly, you must assume, correctly, that there is a fault in the electrical circuit in which the solenoid is situated. Experience has indicated that approximately 85 percent of all hydraulic malfunctions are electrically oriented. The electrical malfunction in directional control valves is generally caused by dirt, which makes a spool immovable, which in turn will cause the solenoid coil to be burned out if it is an alternating current type of solenoid. This holds true in alternating current solenoids only since the inrush current is usually 3 to 7 times the holding current in alternating current circuits. In circuits using direct current on the solenoid coils, the inrush and holding currents are the same; therefore direct current solenoids would not be damaged by midposition stalling of the spool. In the alternating current–type solenoid, if the spool is prevented from moving into the center of the magnetic field that the solenoid coil is producing, the armature is held in the inrush current position, which may or may not burn out the solenoid. If the coil does not burn out, and the coil is overfused, the inrush current may be held on the coil long enough to melt the nylon material on which the coil is wound. The nylon will drop down between the armature and the spool pin extension and harden upon cooling. Even if the stuck spool is removed and cleaned, the nylon material would prevent the power from pulling the armature into position completely. In any event, the valve cannot shift electrically or mechanically. You must change the entire solenoid coil assembly to rectify the situation.

**Step 3: Check Power on the Coil.**   If you hold an allen wrench in the manual override hole, you can usually feel the spool shift as power is applied to the coil. If you push on the opposite side of the solenoid when power is being applied, you may prevent the spool from shifting correctly, and you may cause the coil to burn out. What you have done is prevent the solenoid armature from being pulled in, causing the pull-in amperage to flow at the higher inrush rate. If you can feel the push of the armature— and sometimes you can hear the hum produced by its being held against the inrush current—stop pushing immediately, so that you won't burn out the actuated coil.

If you try to manually override both coils, and you cannot move the spool in either direction, most likely the spool is stuck because of dirt in the bore of the valve holding the spool immobile. Shut the system down. Bleed the system pressure. Loosen both end caps of the valve to get to the pilot spool. This will necessitate the removal of the solenoid housings—and the coils— in order to get at the spool assembly. Remove both of the cover plates gently, so as not to spoil the O rings. Using a brass drift pin, punch the spool free of the housing, making sure that it does not go flying out of the housing or get reversed in position relative to its original position. Using a brass drift pin will eliminate all possibility of causing damage to the bore of the valve or the spool. Clean the spool with mineral spirits. Lubricate it, and reinsert it into the bore of the valve. Be careful not to nick the lands of the spool or bore in the process of insertion. At this time the spool should be free-moving, with but little pressure. Reinstall the side covers, solenoids, and solenoid covers. Start the system and now try to override the valve manually. It should work. This field disassembly can be done regardless of there having been a hydraulic or electrical fault, but you must try to maintain cleanliness. If you can now move the manual overrides in both directions, and the cylinder refuses to work, you must now treat the system as though it were a manual valve, and act accordingly. If you can move the spool with both manual over-rides, and the cylinder works accordingly, you must assume that you have an electrical fault.

If the directional control valve is a solenoid-actuated, pilot-operated valve, the above holds true for testing of the solenoid-operating section. But now there are other factors introduced, because the direct-acting solenoid valve is now supplying pilot pressure to the main spool for the appropriate action.

It is possible for the solenoid valve to be operating correctly, without the appropriate motion of the main spool. The net result is that there is no action of the cylinder. In this instance, you can manually override the solenoid valve and not get operation of the main spool.

**Step 4: Check Main Spool for Tightness.**  If there is no cylinder actuation when you override the pilot spool manually, you must shut the system down and remove both end caps of the main valve. Care must be taken that any residual pressure be relieved from the main valve by loosening the bolts on the side caps just enough to allow flow to occur between the main valve body and the end caps. The best procedure to follow is to loosen those bolts farthest from you first, before you crack those bolts closest to you. Any spray caused by residual pressure will be directed away from you.

When the fluid escapes only by drops, remove both end caps to get at the main spool. Match marking of the end caps may be necessary. Using a brass drift pin, punch the main spool out of the bore of the valve body. Do not let it fly out. Crocus-cloth the spool lightly. Flush the spool with mineral spirits. Lubricate it, and reinsert it in the valve body, making certain that it is in the same relative position as it was when removed. The spool should now "float" in the bore and be easily moved from side to side. If you have erroneously placed it end for end, you will have to do the whole job over, so make certain that you have not rotated it end for end. Reassemble the valve. Turn the system on, and try the manual overrides. The cylinder should work now. If it does not work now, follow the prescribed tests given in steps 3, 4, 5, 6, and 7, as explained in the first part of this section.

For the moment, let us assume that the directional control valve spool was stuck in the bore so tightly that we must scrap the valve and replace it with a new one. Let us further assume that we have a spare valve of the exact nomenclature designation which we are going to install in place of the bad one. We enter a situation which is the same as starting up a new system as far as the replacement valve is concerned. Experience will show you that you must not believe the valve designation. Before you install the valve, you should take the necessary time to check that the valve designation is exactly what it is supposed to be. It is not unheard of for there to be missing or wrongly located plugs in the "innards" of the solenoid-type directional control valves. As we progress from Figure 3 to Figure 4 to Figure 5, you will see how problems can exist which can plague you even on older systems each time that you replace a component with a new one. Casting porosity, loose spool fit, loose spool end plugs, and plugged spool screens are not uncommon.

**Step 5: Check Pilot Pressure and Drain Plugs.**  Figure 3 shows the symbolic arrangement of a double-solenoid, pilot-operated, three-position, four-way directional control valve. The pilot section is solenoid-operated and spring-centered, and it supplies the fluid under pressure to the main spool pilot operators to shift the main spool. The main spool is spring-centered in this case. There are four valve symbols used to show where the plugs may be inserted to accomplish the type of pilot pressure supply and drain. Certain system designs require that the pilot pressure supply be internal or external, and that the pilot drain be external or internal. Most valve manufacturers avail themselves of this potential via the four plugs marked A, B, C, and D. The

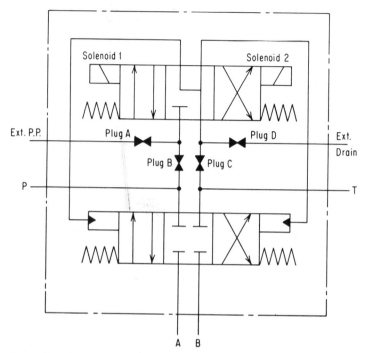

**Fig. 3** Complete symbol of double solenoid–controlled, pilot-actuated, spring-centered directional control valve with external pilot supply and external drain.

following table shows which plug must be in place, or out of place, to achieve the design requirements.

| Pilot Pressure Type | | Pilot Drain Type | |
|---|---|---|---|
| External | Plug A out | External | Plug D out |
| | Plug B in | | Plug C in |
| Internal | Plug A in | Internal | Plug D in |
| | Plug B out | | Plug C out |

If all four plugs are installed in place, actuator function will not occur, since there is no source of pilot pressure available to shift the main spool. This is also true if both A and B plugs are installed. If both C and D plugs are installed, the main spool will shift only once or twice, but never again until the correct plug is removed to allow flow to occur, even if the A and B plugs are correctly located. Let me explain this in detail.

Let us take another look at Figure 1, especially at item 1c. Item 1c is supposed to be internally piloted and externally drained. For this type of valve, we should have plug A installed, and plug B must be out of location. In addition, plug C must be installed and plug D must be out of location. For the sake of argument, let us say that by some quirk of fate someone has failed to remove plug D when the valve was manufactured.

The first time that the no. 1 solenoid is actuated, the system pressure is supplying the pilot pressure, via the pilot spool position, to the left pilot operator of the main spool via the flow path where plug B is absent. The fluid mixed with the air that is in the cavities, will pass through the internal cored holes of the valve to the left side of the main spool. This air-fluid mixture will overcome the spring tension of the right-hand spring and shift the main spool to the right. Because this valve had not been operated previously, there will be air, only, in the right side of the main spool operator. The spool will be shifted to the right, allowing system fluid to go to port A, and opening a flow path from port B to tank. This will allow the actuator to move as desired.

When the no. 1 solenoid is deenergized, the fluid will be pushed out of the left side of the operator for the main spool because of the spring compression of the right side spring. The main spool is now in the neutral position. The flow path of the left side to plug D will be partially pressurized, but with the configuration of the pilot spool, this pressure can also get to the right side of the main spool, since the pilot spool flow path is via the A, B, and T ports.

The second time that the no. 1 solenoid is operated (it is presumed that the no. 2 solenoid is not actuated at all), and only if a very short interval has passed since the first operation, the main spool may shift. If a considerable amount of time has passed, or the spool-to-bore fit of the main spool is loose, sufficient fluid will manage to get to the area where the right centering spring is located, with the result that the main spool cannot be shifted. There is no place for the trapped fluid to go. If the no. 1 solenoid is operated once, followed by operation of the no. 2 solenoid, the main spool cannot be made to shift, since pressure on the right side of the main spool will be the same as the pressure on the left side, and the centering springs will hold the main spool in the central neutral position. The directional control valve is now useless. The pilot spool can be operated electrically or by manual override, and it will move, but no fluid can flow to the main spool or from the main spool because plugs C and D prevent the fluid flow. The valve spool cannot shift.

**Step 6: Check Pilot Plug Installations.** As was stated before, you can run into this problem whether the system is a new one or an old one when you are replacing a bad valve with a new one. Another item which you must check in either instance is whether there are existing external pilot pressure lines or external drain lines. If there is an externally visible drain line, then plug D must be out, and plug C must be in. You cannot, and I repeat, *cannot,* assume that because the nameplate definition of the directional control valve is correct, the plugs are correctly installed or out of location as necessary. Do not forget that this problem can occur with an old system or a new system. One experience of troubleshooting a fault of this type will convince you that you must remember to check the manufacturer's literature for correct plug installation *before* you install the directional control valve. It is so much easier to do the checking at a bench than to do all kinds of contortions out in the field.

**Step 7: Note Pilot Choke Adjustment.** Figure 4 is presented here to show that pilot chokes may be in the circuit between the solenoid valve and the main valve to control the rate of shift of the main valve spool. Unfortunately, the adjustment of the variable orifice can be such as to have no flow from the main spool. If the variable orifice is totally closed, there can be no fluid flow since the check valve also prevents fluid flow. The net effect is that an otherwise perfect valve will not work at all since hydraulic lock will prevent the main spool from shifting. Excessive restriction of the orifice may allow the spool to shift, but prevent it from centering.

As in the case of flow control valves, the direction of rotation of the adjustment screw to achieve main spool travel speed reduction depends on the manufacturer. Some manufacturers' units must be turned clockwise to increase the speed of shift of the main spool, while others must be turned counterclockwise

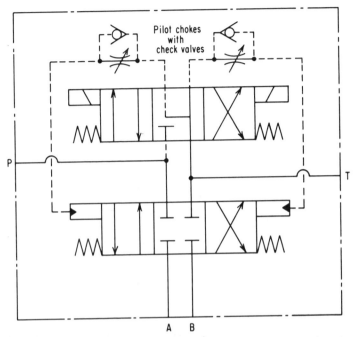

**Fig. 4** Complete symbol of double solenoid-controlled, pilot-actuated, spring-centered directional control valve with internal pilot supply and internal drain plus pilot chokes.

to increase the speed of shift of the main spool. Unfortunately, also, not all manufacturers supply data to tell you which way to turn the adjustment to get the desired effect. You will have to try the adjustment to see which direction of rotation creates the desired effect. These pilot chokes help considerably to reduce the shock which can occur, by gradually opening the flow path for the pilot fluid to pass through. Even spools with throttling grooves can get further antishock capability by the addition of pilot chokes.

**Step 8: Inspect for Pilot Pressure Check Valves.**  In open center directional control valves, where internal pilot pressure is required, as shown in Figure 5, check valve (c) may be employed. The check valve can be in P port of the valve and supply, via internal porting, the necessary pilot pressure to operate the directional

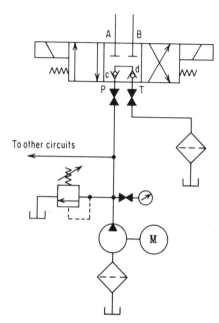

**Fig. 5** Circuit showing directional control valve with locations of internal pilot supply check valves.

control valve. On the other hand, the valve may have no internal porting directly accessible to the pilot valve, and an external tee must then be in the circuit to allow an external pilot supply, via the subplate. The check valve rating must be at least equal to the minimum pilot pressure rating required to shift the main valve spool under design flows and pressures.

Unfortunately, not all of the valve manufacturers' model designations specify the presence of such check valves. Therefore, it may be in existence, but you cannot determine its presence without valve disassembly in many cases.

Some vendors use the check valve in the P port of the directional control valve and others use it in the T port, as shown at (d) in Figure 5, and then only in certain valves and in none of the others. Some vendors do not use this internal check valve arrangement at all. You must check the literature and the valve itself.

Even if all of the vendors made use of a model code designation to indicate the presence of the pilot check valve, one would have to memorize all of the vendors' designation numbers to make certain of the existence of the check valve. This is not too practical.

It is indeed unfortunate that one cannot ever tell for sure by looking at the installation whether there is a check valve in use. There are a considerable number of hydraulic line drawings in existence on which the valve is not even shown.

Spring breakage can occur in these check valves, and when that happens, the pilot pressure will drop below that needed to shift the main spool. You must, therefore, check the catalogs to determine whether a pilot pressure check valve is a part of the directional control valve.

If your testing of the electrically operated directional control valve results in your not having located the fault, repeat steps 3 through 7 for circuits with manual directional control valves.

## Hydraulic Circuit Generalized Faults

Let us go back to Figure 1 again and consider a situation which is not subcircuit in nature, but is a generalized problem. Let us presume that none of the three cylinders function. We must assume, therefore, that we have a generalized fault. The exception to this being a generalized fault would only occur if all of the isolation valves were closed at the same time, or all of the P port isolation valves were closed at the same time, or all of the T port isolation valves were closed at the same time. The first step to troubleshooting a situation of this type, therefore, is to make certain that *all* of the isolation valves are fully open. If all of the isolation valves are fully open, there are quite a few procedures to follow in order to locate the malfunction.

**Step 1: Check Reservoir Fluid Level.**  Check the fluid level to make sure that there is enough fluid available to operate the system. The fluid must be high enough above the pump's suction line to prevent vortexing at the pump suction line. It is safe to assume that the fault lies some place between the reservoir and the isolation valves. Again, it is wisest to make the easiest test first, so go to step 2.

**Step 2:  Check Pressure Gauge Reading at Power Unit.**  Place all three directional control valves in the central neutral position. Start the system. Read the pressure gauge near the pump. Look at your hydraulic line diagram to determine what the correct system pressure should be. Does the gauge reading agree with the line diagram? If the reading is approximately correct, but slightly low, it may indicate a bypassing pump, an incorrectly adjusted pressure relief valve, or some other fault.

If the pressure gauge reading is substantially lower, there are only five items which you must check: (1) the gauge, (2) the pump, (3) the pressure relief valve, (4) the suction filter, and (5) the conduits.

It would be wise to install a known good pressure gauge at this point, and to check that no conduits are crushed.

**Step 3:  Check Pump Drive.**  Check the motor, pump, and coupling to make sure that the pump shaft is rotating. Check further that the rotation of the pump is in the direction indicated on the pump body. A motor may have been changed and wired to run incorrectly. If the motor is running in the wrong direction, have an electrician correct the wiring to correct the rotation. In most instances, running the pump backwards will lead to cavitation, or at least give a noise indication that everything is not normal. You undoubtedly know what the sound of a correctly operating pump sounds like, so this cavitation sound should be recognized. If the pump is running in the correct direction, go on to step 4, the next easiest to do since no disassembly is required.

**Step 4:  Check Pressure Relief Valve Setting.**  Mark the location of the pressure relief valve adjusting screw so that you can reset it to the same point later. Back off the screw, which in most cases will reduce the pressure setting. If in doubt as to the correct direction to turn the screw to reduce pressure, check the manufacturer's component catalog. By backing off the pressure relief valve pressure setting, you are ensuring that most of the dirt on the seat will be washed away by the higher volume flow which occurs at this much lower spring setting. Make sure that you have counted the number of turns you have made so that you can reset the screw to its original point later. Start the pump and allow it to run for a few minutes, then return the pressure relief valve to its original setting. If the dirt on the seat was the cause of the low pressure, setting the valve to its minimum position will cause the seat area to be swept clean by the high volume of fluid passing over the seat. With the lower spring pressure forcing the poppet on its seat, it is much easier for the dirt to be swept away by the fluid flow. Adjusting the valve to its original setting should result in correct pressure gauge reading if the fault was caused by dirt on the seat of the pressure relief valve, and the cylinders should all function correctly now if that was the problem. If the pressure gauge does not read correctly after you have made this test, and the cylinders still function incorrectly, go on to the next step.

**Step 5: Shut Down System and Repair Relief Valve.**    Shut the system down and bleed it of pressure. Multiple actuations of the manual valve should bleed pressure. Without taking any of the pipes apart, remove the appropriate cover of the pressure relief valve. Check the internals as follows:

*Simple Pressure Relief Valve*

*a.* Make certain that the spring is not broken or missing. Replace if needed.

*b.* Make sure that the ball or poppet is in location. If there is no ball or poppet, or it is there but scarred, replace it with the correct replacement part.

*c.* Make sure that the seat is in the correct location and is not scarred. If it is missing or badly scarred, replace it.

*d.* Reassemble the valve, and adjust it to the original setting. You had counted the turns to release the spring setting.

*e.* Start the pump.

*f.* Check the gauge reading.

*g.* If the gauge reads correctly, try one of the cylinders for action. If the cylinder works, you have resolved the problem. If the pressure gauge reads incorrectly, go on to step 6.

*Compound Pressure Relief Valve (Pilot-Operated)*

*a.* Make sure that the pilot spring is not broken. Replace it if it is broken or missing.

*b.* Make sure that the pilot poppet is not broken, missing, or badly scarred. If this is the case, replace it with a new one.

*c.* Make sure that the pilot seat is installed correctly. If it isn't, situate it correctly.

*d.* Make sure that the pilot poppet seat is not cracked. If it is, replace it.

*e.* Remove the pressure relief valve's main spool, poppet, or piston. If it is hanging up due to dirt in the bore, there will be shiny grooves quite visible on it, and these grooves will run along the major diameter. Crocus-cloth the grooves. Flush the part in mineral spirits, and lubricate it with system fluid before reinstallation.

*f.* Check the orifice to make sure that it is not blocked. A blocked orifice in this component will cause the valve to malfunction in the NO PRESSURE mode. Clean the orifice if plugged. Be especially careful to not change its diameter in the cleaning process, or you will change the operating characteristics of the valve.

*g.* Make sure that the main spool, poppet, or piston spring is not broken or missing. Replace the spring as required.

*h.* Reassemble the parts of the pressure relief valve. Start the system pump and check the pressure gauge for correct reading. Try one of the cylinders for operation. If the gauge reads incorrectly, or the cylinder does not function, go on to step 6.

**Step 6: Inspect Pump Shaft Seal**    Note that the checks made so far have required no pipe disassembly. There are two more checks that can be made before any disassembly is required. On some model pumps and some types of pumps, a failure of the pump shaft seal can result in such a loss of pump suction, due to the high ingestion rate of air, that an inadequate suction head is available to induce design flow volumes to the pump. Ordinarily, a failure of this type gives two symptoms which the senses can recognize. First, pump cavitation is caused. The noise produced by cavitation is similar to the sound of a dozen marbles being shaken in an otherwise empty 5-gallon metal container. Second, the air leakage through the seal induces foam production, a milk-colored hydraulic fluid, or both. If the sound of the pump is not normal, you may assume that a bad pump is a part of the cause of your trouble. If inspection of the reservoir fluid shows a milky color to the fluid (and that opaque quality occurs whether the fluid is petroleum, phosphate ester, water-glycol, or most other compositions), the odds are that the pump shaft seal is leaking.

Before you change the pump, there is one more test that you can make. With the pump shut down, apply a liberal layer of grease to the shaft seal area, where the seal meets the shaft. Turn on the pump while you are in the area of the pump and pressure gauge. If there is now a lack of cavitation noise, you have found the fault to be a leaking shaft seal. This pressure recovery would normally be coupled with a correctly reading pressure gauge. The grease has momentarily eliminated the leakage through the seal, and temporarily solved the problem. The pump must be taken off line and the seal *must* be replaced.

If this greasing of the seal area has not eliminated the problem, it may mean that air ingression is from leaking suction piping joints and/or an incorrectly installed filter. With the pump shut down, apply grease to every pipe joint between the reservoir and the pump suction inlet. If this leakage was the fault, the cavitation sound will disappear. If it does, shut down the system, and tighten all of the pipe joints. Start the system again and try the cylinder actuation. If the cylinders operate correctly, you have solved the problem. If the cylinders still fail to work, there is one final check that you can make. Go to step 7.

**Step 7: Inspect Suction Filter.**    Inspect the filter assembly to make certain that it is correctly assembled. Depending on the filter type and manufacturer, it is possible to experience any of the following.

*Cross-Threading of the Cannister.*    It is possible that at the last filter element change, the installer cross-threaded the cannister, which would allow air to enter the system. Correct any cross-threading.

*Incorrect or Leaking O-Ring Seal.*    If there is an O-ring shaft seal on the indicator-of-filter-condition shaft, it is quite possible that this O-ring is leaking air into the pump suction line. Change the seal as required. Some suction line filters have O-rings where the cannister mates with the housing, and this O-ring may have been damaged at the last filter change. Change this O-ring every time that you change the element.

*Loose Filter Housing Mounting Bolts.* Some filters make use of a combination of bolts to hold the filter cartridge retainer in location. Occasionally these bolts are not tightened enough to secure the necessary sealing. The use of the grease application trick can help you find where the error exists.

*Clogged "In-Reservoir"-Type Suction Filter.* All too often, "in the reservoir"-type filter elements are completely forgotten and never changed. When the suction filter is clogged by dirt, the pump starves for fluid, and cavitation naturally results. It is necessary to take the filter out of the reservoir and clean it or replace it with a clean element.

If, after having checked these seven steps, the problem still exists, it must be assumed that the pump itself is at fault. Replace the pump with a known good one, and start up the system (see Section 5). When you replace the pump, you must absolutely align it as per the pump and coupling manufacturers' recommendations, or you will be placing an undesirable load on the pump's bearings, which will lead to seal, bearing, or shaft failure.

Figure 6 shows another system, which differs from Figure 1 only by the existence of cushions on both ends of the cylinders. Let us presume that all of the cylinders function correctly, with the exception of no. 1 cylinder, which does not go to the end of its stroke immediately. People have lived with this type of situation for years without having it corrected.

The rod can extend or retract at rated speed until its cushion spear enters the port block cushion bore, at which time further motion and speed are controlled by the adjustment of the cushion valve. The cushion metering valve can be closed tightly, thus eliminating the full extension or retraction of the rod. If the cushion-spear-to-port-block clearance is small (as it should be for good deceleration control of the cushion valve), leakage through the spear-bore area will be minimal, the rod will not be able to finish its designed travel unless pressure is held on the piston, and slow leakage will occur through the spear-bore area very gradually, with barely noticeable motion of the rod.

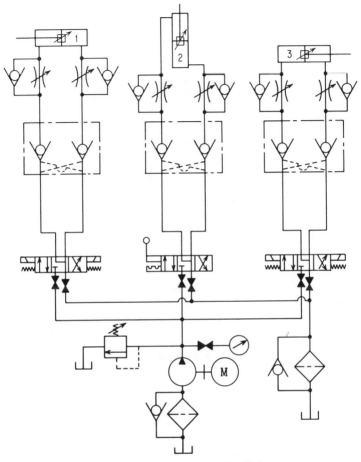

**Fig. 6** Typical hydraulic circuit with cushioned cylinders.

All that is required to eliminate this problem is to back off on the cushion valve adjustment to a position which gives adequate cushioning, then tighten the locking nut. You must be careful that you do not change the valve adjustment while you are in the process of tightening the lock nut.

The potential of this being a problem exists every time that a cushioned cylinder replacement occurs or a new system is started up. Figure 7 shows how the cushion valve can be in the closed

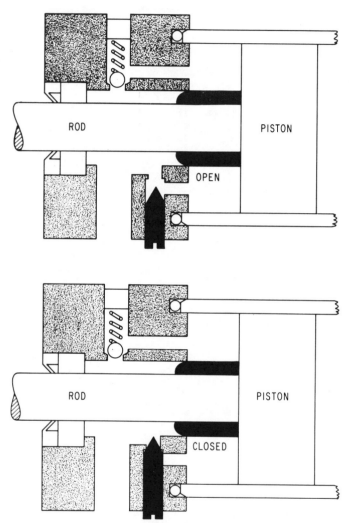

**Fig. 7** Rod-end cushion valves shown in open and closed positions.

position, which prevents the free flow of fluid from the piston side of the port block.

## Reversible Hydraulic Motor Circuit

Figure 8 shows a typical reversible hydraulic motor circuit with crossover relief valves. If the system pressure is set at 1000 psi as viewed on gauge (a), the motor will be able to generate a certain speed and torque as a function of the pump capacity.

There are three types of faults which occur in this type circuit.

**Fault 1: Motor Runs In One Direction Only.** If the unloaded motor runs in one direction only when the appropriate electrical control is energized, you should check the directional control valve by manual override of the solenoid. If the manual override makes

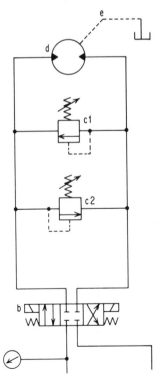

**Fig. 8** Hydraulic motor circuit with crossover relief valves.

the motor operate correctly, there is an electrical fault and the electrician should be notified. If this is part of a multiactuator system, and the rest of the actuators are functional, we must assume that we have a subcircuit fault. It may be necessary to check the directional control valve as explained previously. When you are satisfied that the fault is not in the directional control valve, you can now concentrate on the other components in the subcircuit.

**Step 1: Adjust the Crossover Relief Valves.** With the power off and the system pressure bled, disconnect the hose connections to the hydraulic motor. Plug the ends of the hose with appropriately rated pipe plugs. Start the pump, and increase the system pressure relief valve setting to about 200 to 400 psi higher than it was originally, as read at the gauge, point (a). Manually override the left side of the directional control valve (b), and increase the pressure setting of the crossover relief valve (c-2). If this valve has been tampered with, the pressure reading will increase as you increase the pressure setting of the crossover relief valve. When the gauge reads about 200 psi over what was required to turn the fully loaded motor at design load, lock the adjustment on the crossover relief valve. If the pressure gauge read 1000 psi when the fully loaded motor was correctly operating, then, the crossover relief valve should be adjusted to a pressure gauge reading of about 1200 psi.

Release the manual override on the left side solenoid, and manually override the right side solenoid, making an identical adjustment on the (c-1) crossover relief valve. Lock its adjustment.

**Step 2: Reset Pressure Relief Valve to Correct Pressure.** Now, with the directional control valve in the neutral position, readjust the main system pressure relief valve to its original position, which normally would be between 200 and 400 psi higher than the crossover relief valve settings. The system is now set for the proper operation of the crossover relief valves, and the main system pressure relief valve is also set correctly. What had been happening was that the fluid was preferentially passing over the crossover relief valve rather than turning the motor.

**Fault 2: The Loaded Motor Runs in Neither Direction.** This fault can be caused by the motor having too high a load for the design pressure, or by the crossover relief valves being set too low. If these valves are set too low, the fluid will preferentially pass over the valve and back to the tank without turning the motor. Adjust as indicated previously. If this adjustment does not correct the fault, it is a good indication that the motor is overloaded, or that the motor is worn and bypassing internally. Remove the load to see if the motor will turn when the system is again started up. There is another source for this type of fault. If a common wire is used for the dual solenoid operation, and this is done quite frequently, an "open" in the common wire will result in nonoperation of either of the solenoids, with the result that the motor will turn in neither direction. If the motor turns correctly in both directions of rotation when the solenoids are manually overridden, it undoubtedly proves that there is an electrical fault, and the electrical people should be so informed.

If you think that the motor is worn and bypassing internally, it is quite easy to check on that condition. Disconnect the piping coming out of the case drain (e), and measure the flow into a container for a measured period of time. Check this flow rate against the manufacturer's specifications. Generally, a case drain flow volume of twice the manufacturer's new motor flow rate is enough reason to change the motor.

**Fault 3: Blown Shaft Seal.** The blown shaft seal type of fault is probably the easiest to identify. Fluid is flowing out of the seal and is externally visible. In many cases a frequently recurring problem in many motor circuits is the blowing of the shaft seal. If this happens, invariably the case drain line going back to the tank is undersized. In *every* instance, the case drain line must be at least as large as the case drain port pipe size. If the case drain port size is $^1/_2$ in, the entire run of this line should be no less than $^1/_2$-in *standard* pipe size. There should be no other line feeding into this drainage line, or back pressure can result, causing seal failure. If you run into this seal blowing problem frequently (every couple of months), and the only problem with the motor is the blown seal, you can be assured that the case drain port has been bushed down to a smaller size, and a smaller drain line was used, or else high-pressure pipe was substituted for the standard pipe. The high-pressure piping has a smaller flow area than does the standard pipe. The best solution to this

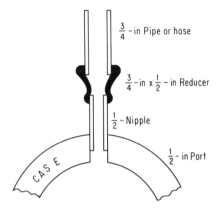

$\frac{3}{4}$ - in Pipe or hose

$\frac{3}{4}$ - in x $\frac{1}{2}$ - in Reducer

$\frac{1}{2}$ - Nipple

$\frac{1}{2}$ - in Port

CASE

**Fig. 9**   Hydraulic motor case drain piping.

problem is to use a short pipe nipple coming from the case drain port, and go to a transition fitting one size larger than the case drain port, as shown in Figure 9.

If your seal leakage problem is infrequent (every 1 to 2 years), it is due to excess wear caused by the normal wear of the motor.

### Pressure-Compensated Pump Circuit

Figure 10 shows another typical hydraulic circuit, less the actuators. The directional control valves $E_1$, $E_2$, and $E_3$ control the various actuators.

With the pressure-compensated pump, all three directional control valves must have blocked P ports, or a check valve in each of the tank ports. The check valves must have adequate spring force to supply high enough pressure if open-port center-type directional control valves are used; otherwise there will be inadequate internal pilot pressure available, and the spool valves could not shift. Some variable displacement pumps, pressure-compensated, use less horsepower at 75 psi and full delivery than they do in the compensated position; hence the need for the check valves to supply the pilot pressure.

Let us presume that none of the actuators function in the system controlled by valves $E_1$, $E_2$, and $E_3$, as shown in Figure 10. To troubleshoot this system you would have to go through the various standard checks as explained previously. When you have satisfied yourself that the problem is general and not sub-circuit in nature, you can now attack the problem by taking the following steps.

**Step 1: Check Compensator and Relief Valve Settings.** With the pump running (you have previously checked that it is running in the correct direction), back off the pump's compensator to see if gauge C has a pressure drop-off. The pressure may remain at the original pressure until you have backed off quite a bit. If that happens, it means that the system pressure is being controlled by the pressure relief valve B, which was set lower than the pump compensator setting. When the system's pressure relief valve setting is lower than the compensator setting, the system

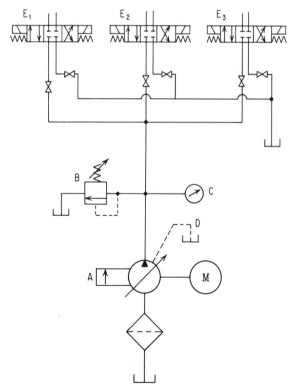

**Fig. 10** Multivalve circuit with pressure-compensated pump.

fluid will overheat, since all of the pump's output is going over the relief valve, at the relief valve setting, and the pump cannot compensate. This setting may be too low to operate the cylinders. If this gauge holding of pressure does occur as you back off the compensator adjustment, you must set the pressure relief valve (B) to a higher setting. Check the drawing and the catalog for maximum safe operating pressure. Turn the relief valve setting in to the design pressure as required, but do not exceed the safe maximum as defined by the literature.

**Step 2: Inspect the Compensator and Readjust.** Start up the system pump. Check gauge C. Slowly turn the compensator adjustor in to achieve the desired pressure. If the pressure does not rise as you are adjusting the compensator, your compensator piston may be stuck, or a flow passage blocked. Shut the pump down. Remove the compensator mechanism from the pump housing, and check for looseness of the piston in the bore. If the piston is binding, you must remove the cause of the binding. Reinstall the compensator and start the pump. With all of the directional control valves in neutral, slowly turn the compensator adjustment in until gauge C reads the design pressure desired. Lock the adjustor in location.

**Step 3: Set Pressure Relief Valve.** In step 1, we set the system pressure relief valve to its maximum position, so that it would not affect the pressure compensator operation. We must now reduce the setting of the main pressure relief valve to a more realistic pressure. With the system running, and all directional control valves in neutral, back off on the system pressure relief valve until the pressure gauge (C) starts to show a drop-off in pressure. This is the point at which the pressure relief valve is controlling the system pressure, because it is not high enough to let the compensator function. When the pressure gauge starts to show this pressure reduction, stop the adjustment of the relief valve. Turn the relief valve adjustor in about one-half to three-quarters of a turn and lock it there. This results in a relief valve setting about 200 psi higher than the compensator setting. You may wish to check the literature on the relief valve for the pressure increase per turn of the adjustor.

There are times when the attempt to adjust the compensator

will result in no effect. Invariably, the compensator spring is broken and it must be replaced.

### Hydraulic Accumulator Circuits

**Leaking Pressure Relief Valve Effect.**    Figure 11 shows a circuit that is used quite frequently, where an accumulator is a necessary part of the circuit.

The pressure switch (a) is usually set to turn the pump on and off at predetermined pressures. The particular circuit is usually used where the frequency of actuator cycling is relatively low. With the use of non-interport leakage–type directional control

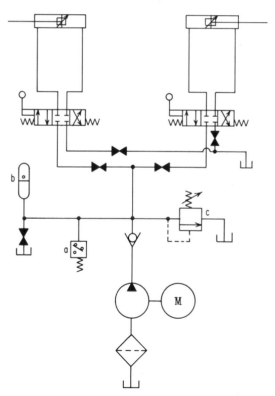

**Fig. 11**  Microswitch-controlled accumulator loading circuit.

valves, the accumulator retains its charge, and is available for
instant use, even with pump shutdown by the pressure switch.
When the directional control valve spool is moved, the accumulator starts to discharge, the pressure reduction being monitored by the pressure switch. The pump is turned on as the
pressure drops to the lower setting of the pressure switch, and
remains on until the switch is satisfied. This is fine *if*, and it is
a big *if*, the pressure relief valve is driptight. If the pressure
relief valve leaks even minimally, and this is especially possible
with certain manufacturers' metal-to-metal seats, then the pump
will cycle at a rate determined by the rate of pressure relief valve
leakage. If this is a small, compact system, the effect of the seat
leakage is much worse than if the system is extensive.

One solution to this type of problem is to get an extremely
large accumulator, thereby creating a larger supply of fluid before leakage would be sensed by the pressure switch. Or get a
pressure relief valve that is equipped with soft seals, which will
considerably reduce the leakage or possibly eliminate the loss
completely.

Figure 12, shows a circuit with an accumulator and a pressure
switch as parts, which is similar to the circuit of Figure 11, except
that in this case the pressure relief valve is mounted before the
check valve and the accumulator. As you can readily see, a non-
driptight pressure relief valve in this location does not affect the
frequency of operation of the accumulator or pressure switch
operation, and therefore this circuit design is to be preferred
over the Figure 11 design.

Problems can still be met within the circuit of Figure 12, though.
Let us presume that the pump is cycling on and off quite fre-
quently, at a rate which is known to be greater than normal.
What can possibly be causing this?

Under normal circumstances, the leakage from the P port of
the directional control valve to the T port is minimal. In most
valves, this would be somewhere in the range of 10 to 40 cubic
inches per minute, with about 1000 psi system pressure. In the
case of Figure 11, this would amount to twice that (two valves),
or 20 to 80 cubic inches per minute. This translates to about
one-tenth of a gallon to one-third of a gallon per minute. If the
accumulator has a 2-gallon capacity (about 1 gallon usable fluid),

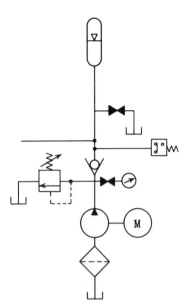

**Fig. 12** Detail of microswitch-controlled accumulator loading circuit with preferred micro-switch location.

the losses through the directional control valves would amount to about 3 minutes of operating time for complete discharge of the accumulator. The pump cycle time due to this leakage would amount to about 3 minutes between complete operations. Suppose that the cycle time were to go to less than 5 seconds. What could possibly cause this to happen? If the accumulator bleed valve to the tank line were partially open, the rate of pressure drop on the accumulator side of the check valve would determine the cycle time of the pump. The greater the degree of opening of the bleed valve, the shorter the time cycle, until such time that a completely open valve would require the pump to run continuously. When short cycle time is noticed, the best first step is to check that the accumulator bleed valve is completely closed. If this short cycle time situation still exists after a check of the bleed valve, you must look elsewhere for the cause of the problem.

**Bag-Type Accumulator.** Consider what would happen if the bag in the bag-type accumulator were to fail. First of all, the nitrogen which was used to charge the accumulator would be contained in the space above the hydraulic fluid, and would alternately be compressed and decompressed as the system is operated. Likewise, there would be a gradual loss of the nitrogen as it went into bubbles in the system and was carried back to the reservoir. Ultimately, there would be no nitrogen above the fluid level, and the accumulator would be nothing more than a standpipe filled with hydraulic fluid. Under these circumstances, the cycle time of the pump would be cut considerably, since the effect of the accumulator would be nonexistent.

**Piston-Type Accumulator.**    In the piston-type accumulator, when the piston seals fail, the nitrogen is pumped into the system, since the system pressure is as high as the nitrogen pressure, and the nitrogen is absorbed into the system fluid. The space occupied by the nitrogen is replaced by system fluid because the fluid leaks past the seals. The piston ultimately moves to its farthest point away from the fluid inlet line. When this occurs, the piston accumulator ceases to be an accumulator and is just a large pipe filled with fluid.

**Accumulator Mounting.**    When the accumulators are mounted so that the flow path of the fluid flow to and from the accumulator is horizontal, the life of the bag- or the piston-type accumulator is seriously shortened as compared with its life if it is mounted vertically.

Water can settle to the bottom of the accumulators when they are mounted horizontally and cause rusting, which in turn initiates destruction of the bag or the piston seals. The piston-type accumulator, when mounted horizontally, is also affected by gravity. The piston has weight, and therefore tends to wear the bottom part of the piston seal much more quickly than if the accumulator were mounted vertically. If space is not a problem, it is to your benefit to mount the accumulator vertically at every installation.

**Cautions.**    On any system which makes use of an accumulator, you must make certain that the bleed valve of the accumulator is opened, and the pressure down to zero, before *any* work is started on any component in the system. Even though the pump is shut down, there is fluid under pressure in the accumulator just waiting for an opportunity to get out. Operation of a directional control valve can cause actuator motion as long as there is some pressure available to do some work.

## Pressure Control Circuits

**Dual-Pressure Circuits.** Figure 13 is a schematic of a typical two-pressure hydraulic system. Let us presume that it is necessary to operate cylinders no. 2 and no. 3 and the hydraulic motor at 900 psi, and cylinder no. 1 at 450 psi. Let us go a step farther and presume that the main system pressure relief valve was bench-set at 1000 psi.

What is wrong with this circuit? Look at it closely because you are bound to run into this situation on more than one occasion.

Examination of the circuit will show you that you would never be able to get the compensator set to the desired 900 psi, since the pressure relief valve, A, is set at 450 psi to control the pressure to no. 1 cylinder. With this setting, it would be set lower than the main pressure relief valve and would therefore be the controlling valve. A pressure relief valve should not be inserted at point A to control the no. 1 cylinder pressure unless the cylinder flow needs are so small that an orifice before the A relief valve would allow the system pressure relief valve to be the pressure controller. The correct location for the pressure relief valve is at point B, unless some other actuator is to be operated simultaneously with the no. 1 cylinder. The correct location for a pressure-limiting device for the no. 1 cylinder is at point B. But, instead of a pressure relief valve, a pressure-reducing valve should be inserted, as shown in Figure 14.

By locating the pressure-reducing valve at point B rather than point A, heat generation by the pressure-reducing valve will be limited to that period of time that cylinder no. 1 is being actuated in the ROD EXTEND mode only. If it were located at point A, the drain line from the pressure-reducing valve would always be passing fluid to tank regardless of whether cylinder no. 1 was being actuated or not.

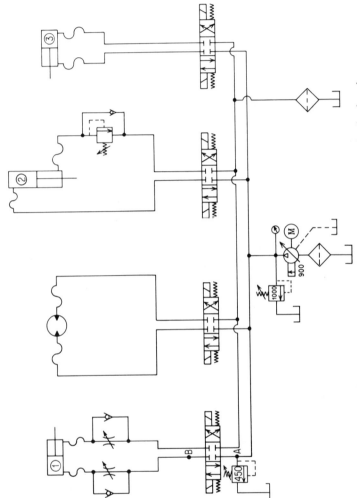

**Fig. 13** Dual-pressure hydraulic circuit showing incorrect pressure control valve location.

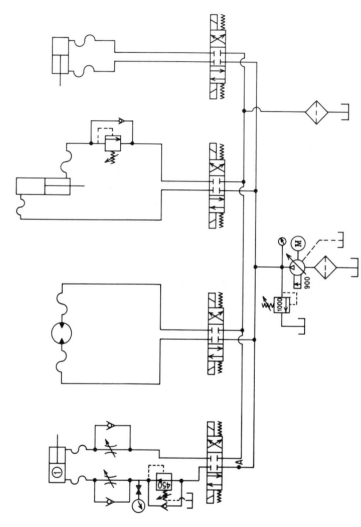

**Fig. 14** Dual-pressure hydraulic circuit showing a preferred pressure control valve and location.

## Pressure-Reducing Valves

Figure 15 shows a circuit making use of a pressure-reducing valve to control the maximum force induced by the cylinder in the ROD EXTEND mode.

Let us consider some of the malfunctions which can occur in this setup, and investigate the causes of the faults.

The piston rod extends, but upon deadheading, system pressure is exerted on the piston. In this case, with gauge b indicating the compensated pressure, gauge c would also show the 900 psi to which the compensator was set.

In the instance that a direct-acting pressure-reducing valve (a) is being used, piston travel can occur. If there is no external

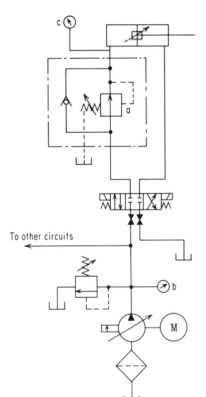

**Fig. 15** Pressure-reducing valve controlling cylinder rod extension pressure.

drain of the spring side of the pressure-reducing valve (a), system pressure will overcome the spring force and allow full system pressure to build up on the downstream side of the pressure-reducing valve. The net result is that the pressure-reducing valve is no valve at all. Reverse full-flow action will not be affected by the lack of the external drain.

In the case of compound pressure-reducing valves, lack of a drain path yields the same result, namely, full system pressure on the cap side of the cylinder. In the event that the pilot valve seat is poor, or the pilot spring is missing or broken, the pressure drop across the main spool will always be high enough to keep the main spool in the position where the downstream pressure will equal the system pressure rather than the preferred reduced pressure.

The problems which arise with pressure-reducing valves generally occur at start-up time, and once the faults are corrected, the valves seem to go on forever without failing.

### Multiple Pump Systems

Figure 16 is typical of the many systems where two pumps must be available due to the critical nature of the application. Pump

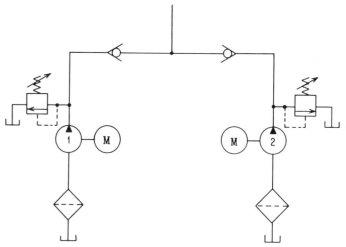

**Fig. 16** Operating and standby pump circuit.

no. 1 is on line, and pump no. 2 is a standby pump. The check valves are isolation checks to allow for maintenance on one unit while the other unit is in service.

Occasionally a malfunction occurs which gives every indication that the on-line pump is at fault when the actual fault is elsewhere. If all of the actuators do not function, a general, as opposed to a subcircuit, fault would be expected. When you run into this situation, you must check, along with correct pump rotation and direction of rotation, whether or not the idle pump is also rotating. Even though the standby pump is off line electrically, it should be checked to see if it is rotating. This is a situation which does not happen too often, but a quick check of the standby pump shaft will tell you if the check valve is bypassing. When this happens, the standby pump will "motor," passing system fluid back to the reservoir, in turn robbing fluid from the system. If the check valve failure is great enough, the fluid loss due to the motoring pump may be enough to prevent actuation of the cylinders and motors in the circuit.

Faults of this sort seem much more prevalent in some of the in-line check valves than in the angle check valves. Installation of rising stem gate valves instead of the check valves will give positive shutoff and eliminate the potential of bypassing check valves completely.

### Counterbalance Valve Circuits

Figure 17 shows a counterbalance valve application. These valves, similar to the pressure-reducing valves in terms of problems, seem to present problems only in the start-up phase of the system. Since most of the component manufacturers use a basic housing with certain variations to change them from pressure relief valves to unloading valves, sequence valves, or counterbalance valves, it is quite possible to have problems with them. The main problem is the orientation of the cover or pilot section of the valve. The internal-external pilot-drain feature is available by the simple rotation of the element to one of four different positions, and the use of or lack of use of plugs to blank off or open up a particular section of the valve. Aside from the possible problem of incorrect location of the bolt-on cover section, the

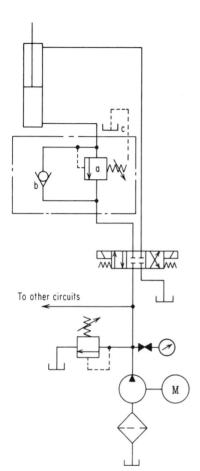

**Fig. 17** Counterbalance valve application.

only problem encountered is the breaking of the spring in those units with internal check valves. Occasionally dirt will hold the check off the seat. Extreme attention to detail must be paid when the covers are installed. Otherwise, a 90 degree rotation of the cover will give you a valve that you did not want. The appropriate O-rings must be correctly installed in the correct locations.

On externally piloted units, one must expect to run into situations in which the pilot pressure supply tubing has been crushed, and the pilot pressure is not available to ensure correct valve operation. One must also expect blockage of the main spool orifice if system cleanliness is not maintained. In addition, breakage of the main spring will prevent the valve from functioning as a counterbalance valve. The unit becomes another piece of pipe if the spring breaks or the orifice is plugged. An orifice is a part of the design of the valve, and it is quite important that system cleanliness is adherred to quite rigorously; otherwise, with a malfunctioning counterbalance valve there can be catastrophic results. Fortunately on-site examination is possible under these circumstances, since the cylinder load will drop, and there will be practically no pressure on the unit. Cautious disassembly is always required if there is a load on the cylinder rod, since there is in effect a weighted accumulator. It is absolutely necessary to shore up the load to prevent any motion in order to do any disassembly of any counterbalance valve.

### Heat Exchanger Circuits

Figure 18 shows a part of a circuit which includes a heat exchanger. In this case, the tank lines from all of the directional control valves join together to send the fluid back through the heat exchanger to tank. If the cylinder, as shown, or any other actuators in the circuit were to malfunction, as might be indicated by a slowdown of the rod speed or a reduction in the available rod force, it would be to your advantage to check the heat exchanger. Every actuator in the circuit would simultaneously show this force reduction or speed reduction since a clogged heat exchanger on the hydraulic fluid side would have the same effect as a variable orifice at the same point in the return-to-reservoir line. As the clearances in the heat exchanger are reduced by dirt, the volume of fluid flowing through it is reduced, and the heat exchanger acts as a meter-outflow control. This is especially true where there is no bypass check valve available in the return-to-reservoir line. In addition to the general slowdown of the actuators, there is another effect. With less fluid flow through the heat exchanger, there is also less cooling effect available for two reasons. This dirt buildup in the exchanger radically affects its efficiency, with less cooling a natural result; therefore there will be a gradual increase in the bulk fluid temperature in the

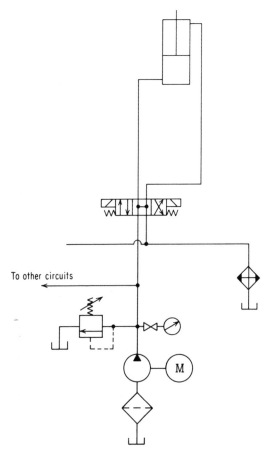

**Fig. 18**  Heat exchanger circuit.

reservoir. This cooling efficiency is further affected by there
being less fluid flow due to the buildup in the exchanger. There
is one additional effect which may or may not be critical to the
circuit. With a dirty heat exchanger there is a larger pressure
drop across the exchanger, and a back pressure to all of the
actuators will occur. This back pressure may not produce actuator problems, depending on how mathematically precise the
system design was. If the designer was conservative with the force
calculation, then there is adequate allowance for such problems

as back pressure in various areas of the circuit. A very positive approach to prevent back pressure from being a problem is to install a check valve around the heat exchanger so that there cannot be a pressure buildup greater than the check valve capability.

Figure 19 shows this arrangement. Introduction of a differential pressure switch across the heat exchanger would help greatly to tell when the exchanger should be taken off line for cleaning.

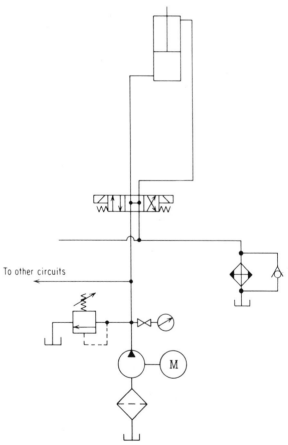

To other circuits

**Fig. 19**  Heat exchanger circuit with check valve bypass capability.

Bypass isolation valves around the heat exchanger would allow you to bypass the heat exchanger while it was out of service for cleaning. Although you would be missing the total cooling effect, you could remove the heat exchanger for maintenance purposes and still run the system, possibly with auxiliary fans on the reservoir. A much better approach is to have a closed-loop system which could include polishing filters in addition to the heat exchanger or exchangers, as the case may be. The polishing filters would extend the service life of the heat exchangers by keeping them cleaner for a longer period of time.

# 4

# NEW SYSTEMS AND START-UP PROBLEMS

As you have seen in the many circuits shown in the previous section on troubleshooting of existing systems, the faults that can present themselves are as many as there are circuits. This section on new systems and start-up problems will show you that there are considerably more problems that can be involved in the new system start-up than in the old established systems. At least in the old established systems, things had been operating. In the new system start-up nothing has been operating at all, and all fault potentials are available. One thing to remember, though, is the fact that each time that you place a new component in an old system, you must treat that particular component as though it were a part in the start-up of a new system. One cannot be emphatic enough relative to not relying 100 percent on the decal or nameplate data on the component. To save yourself time and agony, when time may be at a premium, check the components against the manufacturer's data sheets. You must be certain that you are installing exactly what you think you are installing.

## TYPES OF PROBLEMS

There are about eight things which can happen on start-up which will make you unhappy. They are mentioned in the next paragraph with explanations of the various situations which can cause them, along with suggestions to eliminate the problems.

You will at one time or another run into them, or any of various possible combinations of them at any time. On system start-up, the first thing to be noticed is a pump which is making noise. Or, if there isn't any objectionable noise, the system may not develop pressure, or the pressure may fluctuate. Sometimes, even when the pressure is available, the actuators may fail to move, or they may move in the incorrect direction, or they may move when they shouldn't. They may even move erratically. And, last on the list, the system fluid may overheat. *These problems can also occur with old systems.*

### Noisy Pumps—Causes

Excessive pump noise, or *cavitation* as it is generally called, sounds like a quart of marbles being shaken in an empty 5-gallon container. It is caused by an amount of fluid in the pump chamber which is inadequate to fill the voids between the pumping members. What are some of the causes of cavitation, and how are they cured?

**1. Filter Cartridge or Housing Seal.** If there is a suction line filter installed in the system, and the filter cartridge is installed erroneously, or the seal for the housing is installed incorrectly, there is an air path available for air flow to occur and thus cause cavitation. If the filter has an external indicator, it is quite possible for there to be a missing O-ring at the seal area of the indicator shaft. If the O-ring is missing or is leaking, air gets into the filter and then into the pump suction line. If the cartridge housing is cross-threaded during installation, it is quite possible to get an air leak through this opening.

Examine the filter and make certain that there is no cross-threading of the container. Check that the O-rings are correctly sized and installed in position.

**2. Piping Air Leaks.** Piping air leaks on the suction side of the pump are always to be considered. Every pipe joint, from the suction port of the pump right back to the reservoir, has a habit of leaking regardless of the fitter who installed it. Every pipe joint is a possible leak path through which air can get into the pump inlet and cause cavitation. It is a good idea to go over these pipe joints routinely, tightening those which may have been loosened by vibration.

**3. High Viscosity of Fluid.** If the viscosity of the fluid specified for the system is too high, it is possible to get pump cavitation due to the flow characteristics of the higher viscosity fluid. The fluid will not flow into the pumping chambers fast enough. Clogged piping will give the same results.

**4. Low Temperature of the Fluid.** If the temperature of the fluid is too low on the day that you start up the system, you will invariably run into the problem of pump cavitation until such time that the fluid warms up and the viscosity falls to the correct value. Most pump manufacturers do not want their pumps started when the fluid viscosity exceeds 4000 SUS at start-up temperature. There are some pumps on the market whose manufacturers insist on a maximum start-up viscosity of 500 SUS. It is a very good idea to make certain that the correct viscosity fluid is installed in the reservoir. High viscosity fluid makes it impossible for the fluid to flow into the pump fast enough to fill the pumping chambers and cavitation results.

It is a very good practice to check the component data sheets for the recommended minimum viscosity requirements, and make certain that the hydraulic fluid that will be used for that system will fall well within the recommended viscosity range that is expected for the temperature range that the system will experience.

**5. Incorrect Motor Speed.** A pump which is rotating in excess of its design speed cannot get enough fluid into the pumping chambers, so it cavitates. You must make sure that the motor speed is matched to the pump speed correctly. What are the correct motor and pump speeds? The pump manufacturers specify on their component data sheets what the recommended range of speeds is for each of their pumps. If you exceed the rated speed, you must suffer the consequences of very short pump life. If you are suspicious that the pump speed is too high, it is necessary to take a tachometer reading. Do not think that you can guess correctly what the speed of the rotating shaft is. You can't.

**6. Loose Pump Housing Bolts.** Unfortunately it is not too uncommon to find that the pump was cavitating because there were loose pump housing bolts. These housing bolts must be torqued to the pump body tightly enough, or there will be air leakage paths available, with cavitation being the natural result. Take the time to torque all pump housing bolts to the manufacturer's specifications as shown on the engineering data sheet.

**7. Failure to Prime Pump.** Some pumps, by the very nature of their design, are not self-priming, and it is necessary that the pump casing be filled with hydraulic fluid before the pump is turned over for the *first* time.

The first thing you should do after you have torqued the pump casing bolts is to fill the pump casing with the appropriate clean fluid. This way, you know that the pump is primed properly. Fill the casing through the entry in the top of the pump, and make certain that you replace the plug. It is a good idea at this time to check the manufacturer's brochure for that pump, to determine if it is necessary to supercharge the pump by having a positive pressure in the suction line. This may be quite necessary on pumps which are not self-priming.

**8. Suction Lift Too High.** Pumps have the ability to "pull" only so many inches of suction, and it is possible that the system designer's work may have been done improperly, resulting in too high a "lift" for the particular pump. When this happens you can be certain of having cavitation. The hydraulic fluid cannot get into the pump. If this occurs, it may be necessary to reduce the suction head by eliminating piping or a filter, or else supercharge the inlet to the pump by installing a centrifugal pump which has a flooded suction on it. It may be necessary to elevate the reservoir relative to the main pump if neither of these approaches is possible. Having a flooded suction is one of the best insurance policies against cavitation.

**9. Suction Line Too Small.**  In some instances, the suction line to the pump is too small for the pump. Under these circumstances it is possible that not enough fluid can flow into the pump fast enough. Cavitation results. The suction line for nonsupercharged pumps should never be smaller in size than the suction port of the pump. Generally, it is better practice to go to one size larger and bush down to size right at the pump suction port. For instance, if the pump suction port is $1/2$ inch, use a $3/4$-inch suction line. If the pump suction port is 1 inch, use a $1^1/4$- or $1^1/2$-inch suction line. Make the transition to the suction port size as near as is possible.

**10. Faulty Shaft Seal Installations.**  On some occasions, one gets a pump with the shaft seal installed backwards. The seal is supposed to prevent external leakage of the fluid in the pump. When it is installed backwards, air can enter the pump through the contact area between the pump shaft and the seal. When this happens, a very convenient flow path is available for air to enter the pump and cause cavitation. Never discount this as a possible cause of cavitation. See Section 3, Hydraulic Circuit Generalized Faults, step 6, for tests to do to find this type of fault (page 27).

**11. Short Suction Pipe in Reservoir.**  Another cause of cavitation is to be found in the area of the reservoir. If the inlet pipe to the pump is not submerged beneath the level of the fluid, the pump will get some air into it because there is not enough fluid to fill the pipe. This is caused by poor system design or shoddy installation practices. The pipe must be immersed deeply enough that even with normally low fluid levels there will be enough fluid above the intake pipe to prevent vortexing and air intake. Do not forget that when you filled the reservoir initially, the rest of the system was empty, and some of the reservoir fluid went to fill the voids in the system. Make certain that you top off the reservoir as soon as the rest of the system components are filled with fluid. A good rule of thumb is that the bottom of the suction pipe should be about 6 inches from the bottom of the reservoir, and that there should be a minumum of 6 inches of fluid above the bottom of this pipe, even at low reservoir levels.

**12. High Tank Line Terminations.** One other reservoir area–related problem that can cause pump cavitation is caused by having the return to tank lines terminate above the normal fluid level. When this situation exists, the returning fluid causes aeration of the fluid in the reservoir, since this fluid flows through the air space above the reservoir fluid level and entraps air as it falls into the fluid. This aerated fluid is then carried to the pump suction and causes cavitation. This is especially true when the reservoir is not adequately sized. Incorrect baffles or lack of baffles in the reservoir can lead to these air bubbles being carried to the suction pipe of the pump before the air has had a chance to escape from the fluid. Generally speaking, an adequately sized reservoir would have a total volume in the range of 6 to 10 times the pump capacity in gallons per minute. A 10-gallon-per-minute pump should have a reservoir of 60 to 100 gallons capacity to allow sufficient fluid residence time for the air bubbles to escape from the fluid.

**13. Sticking Vanes in Vane Pump.** Systems using vane-type pumps frequently run into cavitation problems during start-up if the fluid is not clean enough. The particulate matter can cause the vanes to stick in their slots. If the vanes cannot get to the outmost position against the ring, there is a larger space for fluid to fill than normal, and cavitation can result. One of the best procedures to follow in order to prevent this sticking of vanes in the slots is to filter all hydraulic fluid added to the reservoir. One should not even start a system unless the reservoir and piping were cleaned before the introduction of any fluid. Maintenance of a good filter change program also helps.

**14. Pump Shaft Misalignment.** Another cavitation-producing item is caused by the misalignment of the pump shaft with the motor shaft. The slight pump shaft deflection thus encountered is enough, quite often, to cause pump shaft seal deflection and allow air to enter the pump. In addition to this, the misalignment starts to work on the new bearings and causes them to have a short life.

Misalignment is sure to occur if you "eyeball" the alignment. Use the correct tools to align the pump and motor and their coupling. The cost of poor alignment is much more than the cost of the necessary tools to do the job correctly.

## Low or Erratic System Pressure—Causes

You will undoubtedly notice that there is a certain amount of duplication of causes of certain problems, but mention of these causes may be just the gentle reminder you need. Low or erratic system pressure is usually due to one or more of the following causes.

**1. Contamination.** Contaminants in the system fluid can cause sticking or leakage of pressure relief valves and pump compensators, with the net result that the system pressure will rise to the correct level when the unit routinely clears itself of the contaminant, thereby clearing the fault. As soon as additional contaminant prevents the correct setting of the relief valve or compensator from being reached, the pressure drops off again. The frequency of occurrence of this low or erratic system pressure reading can be a function of the particulate matter size and quantity. Keep the system clean if you do not want to be saddled with this problem.

**2. Low Relief Valve Setting.** Another source of low system pressure is too low a setting of the relief valve. In a correctly designed system, where the relief valve is adequately sized, the system pressure should never exceed the maximum setting of the relief valve. If the valve is too small for the speed (gallons per minute) of the pump, it is possible to get the system pressure over the true setting of the relief valve, and blow up the weakest component in the system. In a correctly designed system, it is possible to have a factory-set pressure relief valve set to a pressure lower than the one specified on the drawing, or someone may have adjusted the valve to a lower point than the drawing called for. In that event, the fluid from the pump will be going over the relief valve and back to tank without building up to the required pressure.

**3. Wrong Compensator Setting.** If the system makes use of a compensated pump with a system pressure relief valve and the compensator setting is too low, system pressure will then be determined by the setting of the compensator, but only if the system relief valve is set higher than the compensator setting. If the relief valve is set lower than the compensator setting, then the relief valve will be the determinant of the system pressure. Normally, the system pressure relief valve is a safety valve to protect the components in the event of compensator failure. In the instance in which the system pressure relief valve is set lower than the compensator setting, the pump can never go into the compensated mode. If there is no system pressure relief valve, the compensator will be the determinant of the system pressure. An incorrect setting of the compensator will result in an incorrect system pressure. Don't forget the fact that most compensated pumps that you get are *not* set at your desired pressure. You must set them at the pressure which you desire.

**4. Low Crossover Relief Valve Setting.**   Some systems make use of crossover relief valves, and regardless of their purpose and regardless of the presence or absence of a pressure-compensated pump or system pressure relief valve, if the crossover relief valve setting is lower than the pressure necessary to move the load, the system pressure will never exceed the setting of the crossover relief valve. The fluid will bypass the actuator and go back to tank by means of the crossover relief valve. This valve must be set higher than the anticipated pressure required to move the load or it will not move, and the system pressure will equal the crossover relief valve setting. It usually pays to take the time to bench-set the required pressure on the crossover relief valve before piping it into the system.

**5. Low Reservoir Fluid Level.**   Low fluid level in the reservoir can result in low or erratic system pressure. The pump does not always get enough fluid to fill the pumping cavity; in this case only a small amount of fluid is discharged into the system, with a resulting drop-off of pressure, since some air is also introduced into the piping. Frequent check of the reservoir fluid level gauges will be quite helpful in remedying this problem. Fill the reservoir to normal operating levels with filtered fluid only.

**6. Reversed Shaft Seal.**   A symptom similar to that caused by low fluid level in the reservoir is that caused by pump shaft seals installed backwards. Air gets into the pumping cavity and is sent out into the system, resulting in low or erratic system pressure.

## No System Pressure—Causes

There are a variety of things which can lead to there being no system pressure, and they can occur singly or in combination with other causes.

**1. Low Reservoir Fluid Level.**   If the liquid level of the fluid in the reservoir is below the level of the pump's suction line, there is no possible way for the fluid to get to the pump and thus out into the system to produce the pressure effect. Too many reservoir liquid level indicators are situated at a level too high in the reservoir to give a readable level indication. It becomes necessary to take an accessory out of location on the reservoir in order to peek into the interior to check the fluid level. All too often during this inspection, dirt is introduced into the reservoir.

**2. Wrong Direction of Pump Rotation.**   If the pump motor is turning in the wrong direction of rotation, the pump cannot generate fluid flow in most instances. It is necessary that the correct pump rotation be checked early in the system start-up.

**3. Missing Coupling Key.**   There are a few occasions when the pump-to-motor coupling key is omitted during the setting up of the pump, so even though the motor is rotating, the coupling may or may not rotate, and the pump definitely will not rotate. Without the pump rotating there can be no flow, and without flow there can be no pressure buildup. Take the time to check that the coupling and the pump shaft are rotating.

**4. Incorrect Pressure Relief Valve Setting.**   On some system installations, the system pressure relief valve has been backed out to the minimal pressure setting, and may even have all of the spring force removed from its actuation position. The net effect is minimal pressure or just line pressure, brought about by the frictional resistance of the piping components.

**5. Incorrect Compensator Pressure Setting.** A compensator-type pump may have an identical situation arise, again with a minimal pressure showing on the gauge.

**6. Incorrectly Assembled Pump.** An incorrectly assembled pump will usually result in there being no system pressure since no fluid is flowing into the system to create pressure.

**7. Incorrect Component Assembly.** Other system components can be erroneously assembled, with the result that the fluid can flow back to the reservoir without there being a buildup in pressure. Directional control valves can have their spools inserted in the bore in the wrong direction, giving a pressure-to-tank flow path which would result in a no-pressure or low-pressure condition.

**8. Broken Fluid Conduit.** A broken pipe, hose, tubing, or fitting in the main line of the system will lead to a no-pressure condition. Fortunately, in most instances, these types of failures are readily visible and can be corrected quickly.

**9. Broken Gauge.** A broken gauge can give a wrong pressure reading and indicate no pressure even though the pressure may be correct. Bench testing of all of your pressure gauges can eliminate this type of problem.

### Actuator Fails to Move—Causes

For a hydraulic system to function correctly it is necessary that the actuator move at the rated speed, with the correct pressure available to produce the desired force in the correct direction. Unfortunately there are probably more causes for no motion of the actuator than for most other types of malfunctions, as you will see by the following list.

**1. Incorrect Component Assembly.** On some occasions, though rarely, the actuator is assembled incorrectly, or there are some parts missing from it. For instance, the locking mechanism which holds the piston on the rod of a cylinder may be missing, and the rod cannot retract. If this is the case, there is no possible way for the rod to retract. In some instances, the absence of seals, or seals installed backwards, can lead to failure of actuator motion. A large external leakage can result in failure of the actuator to move. Fortunately, though, this is rather easy to spot in most instances. The most difficult faults to troubleshoot are those wherein the internal leaks occur.

**2. Malfunctioning Pump.** A malfunctioning pump, regardless of the cause of the malfunction, can lead to lack of actuator motion. If no gallonage is being produced, there can be no actuator motion. As was mentioned previously, there are quite a few reasons why pump malfunction will lead to such nonflow conditions. Lack of keys in the coupling, pump running backwards, parts missing, pressure plate reversed, pressure compensator stuck or set too low, pump shaft failure, and a few other items are included in this pump malfunction category. Component disassembly is required to locate this fault.

**3. Directional Control Valve Faults.** Directional control valves are probably the leading cause of lack of actuator operation. Listed below are some of the faults which are factors in malfunctioning of the directional control valves, which in turn affects the actuator motion.

*Low Voltage.* Low solenoid coil input voltages result in initiation of the shifting of the armature, but the voltage is not high enough to produce complete armature motion, so the armature is returned to the home position (deenergized position) by the spring. The armature is again shifted with the same repetitive results. The spool is never shifted to the desired final position; therefore there is no movement of the actuator. In most instances, in a 120-volt alternating current system, if the voltage falls below about 92 volts, as measured at the coil wires, there is just not enough voltage available to complete shifting of the armature of the solenoid. The unit sounds like a machine gun, but nothing happens to the actuator. When the voltage falls below about 90 volts, there is no armature pull-in at all. If the wire gauge is too small for the length of run of the wires from the control cabinet to the solenoid coil, there will not be enough voltage available for the shift to occur completely. The solenoid armature will shift from the neutral position to a partially shifted position and back again, but the hydraulic actuator will not move.

Solenoid indicator lights are a great aid in determining a malfunction of this type.

*Power Loss.*   Electrical power failure in the particular directional control valve circuit can be a short in the wires leading to the solenoid coil, an "open" in the wires, a burned-out fuse in that circuit, or a fault induced by a limit switch or control circuit relay of that particular circuit. If the solenoid coil has overheated, it is possible for the nylon portion of the coil winding support to melt down between the armature and the spool extension, so that the spool cannot be shifted.

*Spool Binding.*   If spool binding occurs in the pilot spool or the main spool, even though the electrical circuit requirements are met, it is impossible for the spool to shift. If the main spool does not shift, the actuator cannot move. If the pilot spool cannot shift due to binding, two things can happen. If the pilot spool cannot shift, the main spool, which is controlled by the pilot spool, cannot shift, and the actuator cannot move. If the pilot spool does not move, and the solenoid is an alternating current type, the coil will burn out, since the inrush current will be applied constantly. The inrush current is about 3 to 7 times the holding current. Fortunately, this is not a problem in direct current applications, where the inrush and holding currents are the same, and the coils are designed for this current load. The spool binding can be caused by dirt preventing the spool motion, but it is quite possible that the bolts holding the pilot section of the valve to the main valve body have been overtorqued. In this instance, with many manufacturers' units, it is possible to bind the spool in the bore of the pilot valve. It is imperative that the body bolts be torqued to the vendor's specifications as shown in their literature on the particular valve.

*Incorrect Valve.*   Occasionally, the incorrect valve is supplied for the particular application. A two-position, two-way valve with the solenoid mounted on the incorrect side of the valve can result in a no-flow mode when the coil is energized. If this happens, there can be no actuator motion, since the flow path will be blocked by the spool.

*Closed Pilot Chokes.* On compound directional control valves, those valves which use solenoids to control the shift of the main spool, it is quite possible to have inadequate pilot pressure or a lack of a flow path available for the main spool to be shifted. If there are pilot chokes (variable flow control devices) in the valve to control the speed of the main spool shift, and the chokes are completely closed, hydraulic lock can prevent the shift of the main spool. If the main spool does not shift, the actuator cannot move. Even if the pilot spool moves correctly, the main spool cannot move since a flow path ceases to exist.

Check the hydraulic drawing and the manufacturer's literature as well as the physical installation to be certain that the pilot supply and drain are as designated. If there aren't any external conduits for external pilot supply and/or drain, the valve cannot work correctly. See Section 3 and Figures 3 and 4.

*No Pilot Pressure.* In a compound directional control valve, a lack of pilot pressure will produce the same results as a lack of electrical power to the solenoid. The fluid is not at a high enough pressure to cause the main spool to shift into the correct position to get motion of the actuator. Make certain that you have adequate pilot pressure.

**4. Mechanical Binding.** If there is mechanical binding in the mechanical circuit which the actuator is trying to move, there will not be adequate system pressure to overcome this excess frictional resistance, and the actuator will not move. You must remove the load on the cylinder to determine if there is a mechanical binding. On some occasions it is necessary to disconnect the actuator from the linkage and attempt to get motion.

**5. Lack of Proper Actuator Seals.** Lack of adequate sealing in the actuator, whether it be a cylinder or a hydraulic motor, leads to internal leakage, which at times can be great enough to prevent correct pressure buildup in the actuator. The net result is no actuator motion. Wrong piston seals or seals too soft for the pressure can lead to gross internal leaks with resulting lack of actuator motion.

**6. Incorrect Piping.** Incorrect piping of the directional control valve can result if the pressure piping is installed into wrong port of the valve. The same holds true if the two actuator ports are switched in their piping. Extreme care at the time of piping installation must be taken to be sure that the valves are piped correctly. Switched hoses at the actuator can produce the same effect.

**7. Directional Control Valve Springs.** If certain of the springs in the directional control valve are missing, broken or weak, a condition can occur wherein there can be no flow to the actuator, and the actuator will not move.

**8. Directional Control Valve Mounted Incorrectly.** The directional control valve can be mounted backwards on the baseplate and one cannot expect the actuator to work under these circumstances. The ports in the baseplate must align with the ports in the valve body. You may have to remove the valve from the baseplate to determine this.

**9. Missing Pilot Line on Pilot-Operated Check Valve.** Actuators in circuits with pilot-operated check valves can only move in one direction if the pilot line is not piped into the check valve. The fluid can flow in the free flow direction only, and since there is no pilot pressure available to lift the poppet off its seat, reverse flow through the check valve is impossible. In the event of dual pilot-operated check valves, it is almost impossible for this malfunction to occur without there being serious dirt contamination of the pilot spool or piston.

**10. Incorrect Piping of Valves.** Actuators in circuits with sequence valves or counterbalance valves may not work properly if these valves are piped incorrectly. If the "in" piping is attached to the "out" line of the valves, there can be no flow, with the result that the actuator does not move.

## Actuator Moves in Incorrect Direction—Causes

**1. Directional Control Valve Spool Mounted Backwards.** On certain manufacturers' valves, and only on certain of their models, it is possible to have the spool reversed in the bore of the valve and end up with the actuator moving in the incorrect direction. If the valve model is one with all ports plugged in neutral, and the spool is reversed, the valve will function correctly in the neutral position, but will cause the actuator to move in the incorrect direction when it is actuated.

**2. Solenoid Wiring Reversed.** The electrical wiring for the directional control valve must be correct. The A solenoid wires cannot be attached to the B solenoid and have the actuator move in the correct direction. The B solenoid wires cannot be wired to the A solenoid coil without there being reverse operation of the actuator. Check the electrical ladder diagram for wire numbers and make certain they are in agreement with the way that the drawing calls for the wiring to be done.

**3. Directional Control Valve Piping Reversed.** If the A port piping is installed in the B port of the directional control valve, the actuator will move in the incorrect direction when the directional control valve is actuated. In most instances, the ports of the directional control valves and the baseplates for the directional control valves are appropriately marked as to which port is which. The piping arrangement should be in accord with the hydraulic line diagram. You may have to trace the lines to the actuator to detect this type of piping error.

**4. Actuator Hoses Reversed.** The actuator hoses must be correctly attached to the actuator for the actuator to move in the correct direction. Hooking the A port hose to the B port of the actuator will naturally cause movement of the actuator in the incorrect direction.

### Actuator Moves When Not Desired— Causes

**1. Back Pressure in Circuit.** Back pressure can result when various subcircuits discharge into a common line which is not sized large enough for the various flows into it. Depending on the directional control valve's neutral flow path, certain circuit designs can cause this back pressure to cause actuators to move when they should be held in a stopped position. This is especially true of unloaded motors and cylinders. Installation of check valves can eliminate this, but the spring force of the check valves must be low enough to not otherwise affect operation of the system.

**2. Incorrect Solenoid Location.** Two-position directional control valves with the solenoid mounted on the incorrect side will result in actuation when the solenoid is deenergized, if the flow paths are functional at the time. If the hydraulic line diagram calls for the solenoid to be on the A side of the valve, it must be mounted there for correct actuator motion.

**3. Transient Currents.** In servo systems, it is possible for transient currents to actuate a servo valve by placing a voltage of either polarity on the torque motor, which in turn will cause the actuator to move. The torque motor does not know that it has received a false signal, so it follows the signal input and reacts accordingly.

## Slow or Erratic Actuator Operation—Causes

Slow or erratic operation of the actuator can be caused by a considerable number of things. Listed below are but a few of them.

**1. Air in Fluid.** Air in the fluid to the actuator causes a spongy type of motion of the actuator. Generally, the motion is a slipstick type of movement, quite similar to the motion of an elevator when it stops at a floor. The air in the system is causing this to happen. The cylinder rod moves because enough pressure has been generated to cause the motion, but with the motion, the air in the cylinder expands because there is now room for that expansion to occur. Additional fluid is introduced into the cylinder and recompresses the air to the correct pressure to cause further motion. The greater the amount of air, the greater will be the sponginess of the actuator motion. If the end of the suction pipe in the reservoir is not sufficiently submerged in the fluid, vortexing of the fluid will occur, with a pickup of air resulting. Make certain that there is enough fluid in the reservoir, and that you have no suction pipe leaks.

**2. Wrong Fluid Viscosity in System.** The viscosity of the fluid charged into the reservoir must meet the requirements of the pump manufacturer. If the viscosity is too high, the fluid velocities will be adversely affected, and slowdown of the actuators will occur. A similar condition will exist at start-up if the temperature of the fluid is so low as to result in the viscosity of the fluid increasing beyond the specifications of the pump manufacturer. This is a serious problem which can lead to pump cavitation. The appropriate solution is to replace the fluid with the correct one.

**3. Internal Leakage in Actuator.** Internal leakage in the actuator will, regardless of the cause, result in fluid bypassing internally, with slowdown of the actuator being the natural result.

**4. Clogged Suction Filter.** A clogged suction filter without bypass capability will result in a reduction of fluid to the pump, and a reduction of fluid to the actuator. Naturally, the actuator will operate more slowly. This is one of the prime reasons for making use of indicating-type filters, and not using filters which are inside the reservoir.

**5. Incorrect Component Sizing.** If the pump is not sized large enough to give the design speeds to the actuator, the speed of the actuator cannot possibly be as fast as originally calculated. If the actuator is larger than necessary for the function it is performing, the pump cannot make it move at the rated speed.

**6. Wrong Motor Speed.** If the speed of the pump is different from the speed used in the original calculations, the pump will be producing less flow for a slower electric drive motor and more flow for a faster electric drive motor. Industrial hydraulic pumps are positive displacement units, and their outputs are directly proportional to the speed of rotation.

**7. Motor Speed Too High.** A pump which is being driven at a greater speed than its design rating may cavitate, and a reduced volume of fluid will then be available to the actuator, resulting in slower actuator speed.

**8. Motor Wired Incorrectly.** If the pump is installed with the electric motor causing it to run backwards, there may be no flow or a very minimum of flow, with resulting slowdown in actuator speed. In order to correct the direction of the motor rotation it is necessary to switch certain of the leads of the motor. With certain types of direct current motors, reversal of the motor leads at the main disconnect instead of at the motor can result in an extremely high rotational speed of the motor. Although this reversal has corrected the direction of pump rotation, the motor without the pump coupled to it would tear itself apart through overspeeding. With the pump coupled to it, the pump acts as a brake and prevents the extreme overspeed from occurring. The pump would at that time be running way over its rated speed and cavitation would occur. All wire changes to correct incorrect direction of rotation of electric motors should therefore be done at the motor, not at the main power disconnect.

**9. Mechanical Binding.** Mechanical binding can lead to slowdown of the actuator. Sticking, warped, binding of the mechanical elements can cause this to happen. The quickest test for this is to disconnect the cylinder or motor from the load and see if the actuator can be operated with no load on it.

**10. Sticking Directional Control Valve Spool.** A valve spool which has only partially shifted due to contaminants in the bore-to-spool area can result in a throttling effect which would cause the actuator to move slowly. If the valve-to-base plate bolts on one side are tightened too much, the spool may only shift partially, and interport flow, which is meter-off in nature, will result in the actuator only getting part of the pump's output.

**11. Internal Leakage in Pumps and Other Components.** Worn components or low fluid viscosities will allow for an increase in the amount of internal leakage in the various components. If the pump bypass is increased by the wear, or by too low a fluid viscosity, the amount of fluid that is available for actuator movement must be reduced, with a slowdown of the actuator being the natural result. A frequent check on the temperature of the fluid in the reservoir and the amount of case drain leakage of the pumps will help to tell you where the problem lies.

**12. External Leakage.** An external leak in any part of the system is the same as a meter-off flow control situation. Part of the fluid which would normally be available for moving the actuator is not available due to this fluid loss. In a few instances it is possible to have this external leak be not too visible due to the design of the system. Mechanical design may make the leak difficult to find due to the way that pipelines are routed into places which are difficult to see. Constant surveillance is necessary to catch this. Frequent checking of the fluid level certainly helps.

## System Overheats—Causes

Practically any system will end up with an elevated bulk system temperature if the reservoir is too small to adequately disperse the excess heat in the fluid. If the reservoir must be made smaller than optimum size, it becomes necessary to install a heat exchanger in order to keep the fluid's temperature, and its viscosity, in a reasonable range. An air-to-fluid heat exchanger, with forced fan cooling, or a water-to-fluid type may become necessary when ambient temperatures encountered are not low enough to generate the desired amount of cooling effect. Even with a large enough heat exchanger, there can be malfunctions which can result in an increased fluid temperature.

1. **Water Supply Too Hot.** The cooling water to the heat exchanger must be within the temperature range for which the exchanger was originally designed. If the water temperature is above this cooling fluid design temperature, the cooling effect will be reduced. If the cooling water is not turned on, there can be but a minimal cooling as a result of the conduction, radiation, and convection of heat by the shell of the exchanger alone. Frequent checking of the temperature indicator in the inlet line of the cooling fluid will tell you if this condition exists.

2. **Low Volume Flow of Hydraulic Fluid.** The valves which control the flow of hydraulic fluid into the heat exchanger must be open. In addition, any isolation valves at the hydraulic fluid exit of the heat exchanger must be fully open. Having just the cooling water valves open will accomplish nothing if the hydraulic fluid cannot get into the area where the cooling can take place. A partially closed isolation valve is a flow control device, and as such will restrict the amount of cooling which can occur.

3. **Dirty Exchanger.** A dirty or clogged exchanger cannot possibly produce the same amount of cooling effect that is possible with a clean unit. Installing a used heat exchanger in a new system is very poor practice unless the unit has been thoroughly cleaned and tested before installation.

**4. Stuck Compensator.** A compensator-type pump which has a stuck compensator at an undesirably high pressure can cause a high temperature in the reservoir, even with a new pump.

**5. Improper Spool Shift.** When a system makes use of a directional control valve as a part of a pump unloading scheme, and the valve spool does not shift completely, regardless of the reason there will be a temperature rise in the fluid in the reservoir since the pressure drop across the partially shifted spool valve will, with the leaking of several gallons per minute of fluid, generate heat.

**6. Incorrectly Seated Relief Valve.** If the system's pressure relief valve is not seating correctly, there will be an internal leak which will result in extra heat going into the system since there is a flow path from the high pressure area to the low pressure area.

**7. Incorrect System Design.** When a system is designed so that it is possible for a piston rod to travel to the end of the stroke whether extended or retracted (deadheaded position) and stay in that location while fluid passes over the relief valve, there must be an increase in the fluid temperature. The system design must be such that a limit switch shifts the valve spool or the pump must go to an unloaded position, either by limit switch or pressure switch unloading, or some other accepted practice.

**8. Internal Leakage.** When system components wear to the point that internal leakage occurs, whether it be a pump, motor, or other actuator, there is bound to be an increase in system temperature due to this leakage. The higher the rate of leakage, the higher will be the temperature increase in the system.

**9. Improper Reservoir Positioning.** One can have a correctly designed system and reservoir, and still end up with temperature elevation in the reservoir. There must be adequate air circulation availability for the reservoir to contribute to the cooling effect. If the reservoir is set flush on the floor, effective cooling area is being made unavailable. There must be adequate side clearance all around the reservoir for the walls of the reservoir to be cooled by ambient air. Hiding a reservoir too close to concrete walls will certainly decrease the available cooling effect that could be attained if there were some space for air circulation.

As you can see from the foregoing, problems can be legion. This is definitely not limited to the start-up of a new system. Similar problems can arise when any hydraulic component is changed in a system. You must assume that the new component is not exactly the component you expected to get. The literature supplied by the component manufacturer must be checked every time that you install a new component in the system. You must physically check for the presence or absence of the various plugs, springs, pistons, etc., before you install the component in the system, to forestall having to remove it because it did not do what it was supposed to do.

## TROUBLESHOOTING PROCEDURES

As you have learned in the previous sections, a considerable number of things can go wrong, and an even greater list of items contribute to hydraulic system problems. The trouble with a new system is that you have had no previous experience on it, and you must expect to have problems with this new system.

### Pre-Start-Up Procedures

Troubleshooting of new systems at start-up is usually a very disconcerting situation unless you preplan the job. You are invariably confronted by a large work force of most of the craftspersons, upper echelon operating personnel, and upper echelon maintenance personnel, all of whom are in a hurry to get the system on line and functioning. It can be a very nerve-racking situation, but you can make it almost agreeably pleasant if you prepare for it. This preparation must be instituted while the system is being installed because you cannot do all of the preparation on the day of the start-up.

There are a few items which must be done as soon as all of the components and piping are installed in location.

**Step 1: Clean System Before Adding Fluid.**  The entire system must be cleaned, flushed, and prepared for start-up. See Section 6 on Cleaning and Flushing.

**Step 2: Check Components For Correct Installation.**  You *must* trace the entire system to make sure that the components are installed as stated on the line diagram, with all flows in the correct direction, and all ports piped correctly. You cannot assume that the people installing the equipment have done the job correctly. Check the component identification tags against the hydraulic line diagram and/or bill of materials for the job. Pay particular attention to the nomenclature of the digits of the components. Make certain that they are in *complete* agreement with the diagram. Correct any mistakes before start-up.

**Step 3: Fill Reservoir With Correct Fluid.** As soon as you have completed steps 1 and 2, fill the reservoir to within 1 inch of the top with the appropriate fluid. Most of the fluid in the space above the normal operating fluid level will be used to fill the lines and the various other components in the circuit when you go through the various actuator operations. Pay particular attention to making sure that you are putting clean fluid into your system. If there are many accumulators or large accumulators in the system, you must make certain that you leave space in the reservoir for their drain-back. When filling the reservoir, it is to your particular advantage if you pump the fluid through a 10-micron filter. This will assure you that you are dealing with a known clean system at start-up.

**Step 4: Check Filter Elements.** Check that all the filter elements are in location. This means disassembly of the case to actually see the cartridge. Be sure that you have at least six spare elements on hand for each throwaway element in the circuit. If you have cleanable elements in the filter case, it would be appropriate to have at least one spare on hand, so that you do not have to shut the system down while cleaning the dirty unit. It is quite appropriate to change each filter within the first 24 hours of operation of the system. This original element will pick up contaminants missed by your cleaning and flushing operation, and is very cheap insurance. It is even wiser to change all of the elements after the first hour of operation, and again after 24 hours.

**Step 5: Set Pressure Adjustment.** Set the main pressure relief valve, pump compensator, and all pressure-controlling valves to the minimum pressure point. This includes sequence valves, counterbalance valves, crossover relief valves, unloading valves, etc. By making these settings, you are making certain of getting the maximum flow rates with the minimum pressures available. Invariably, none of the settings is correct anyway, so you might as well start out with everything in your favor. It is presumed that all over-center loads would be at the bottom of their stroke because of the installation. If this is not the case, it is necessary to set all counterbalance valves at their maximum pressure setting in order to prevent falling of the load. In any event, you will be setting each valve to the correct pressure setting later, after you have sustained flows from the pump.

**Step 6: Adjust Speed Controls and Cushion Valves.** Open every cylinder cushion valve to the midpoint of its travel, and adjust every speed control to its midpoint of travel. By doing this you are assuring yourself of some flow capability. They will all have to be set correctly when you fine-tune the system.

**Step 7: Fill Pump Casing with Correct Fluid.** Fill all pump casings with the appropriate clean hydraulic fluid, making certain that you maintain maximum cleanliness during the process. Make sure that you replace the plug that you removed to add the fluid. Prefill all accumulators to the appropriate pressure with nitrogen. Have an electrician "bump" the motor to be certain the motor is turning in the direction of the arrow on the pump casing. If the motor direction is incorrect, have the electrician change wires and retest for correct motor rotation. As mentioned previously, this change must be made at the electric motor and not at the main disconnect switch. Break all cylinder and hydraulic motor connections, and move the cylinder rods to safe positions, as well as turning the hydraulic motors to their safe positions. This places all of the actuators in positions which would not be harmful at the time of start-up. Manually override *every* directional control valve, electrically and mechanically actuated, to make sure that they are free to move. As noted previously, sometimes the valves are bolted to the baseplates so tightly that the spools cannot be shifted. If you cannot manually shift any directional control valve, make sure that you loosen the bolts and torque them to the manufacturer's specifications.

**Step 8: Have Maintenance Personnel Available.** Make arrangements to have two mechanics and two electricians available to you for the entirety of the start-up day, or until you release them.

Having completed these eight items, you are ready for start-up day. You have made all of the arrangements that should be made to be hydraulically ready. One additional step may be taken if you want to make certain that start-up will run smoothly. Get an electrician or an electrical foreman assigned to you the day *before* start-up. Have the electrician manually override every limit switch in the circuit which may affect your hydraulic equipment. Make certain that your electricians check, in the motor control center, that all electrical switches are wired correctly, and that includes filter bypass electrical signal elements. If any of the electrical items are wired backwards, it is quite possible that they will be permissive in nature and prevent your start-up.

By following all of these eight steps in advance, you will have eliminated most of the small things which would normally be plaguing you on the day of start-up. You will now be allowed to concentrate fully on getting the unit on line and operating the way it was designed to operate.

On extensive systems you may find it worth your while to make a checkoff list of all the components, and go over the list, item by item, to make sure that you have covered them all. Another approach that may work even better is to take a spare print of the hydraulic line diagram along with you, and color off in red or brilliant yellow those components which you have personally checked for the appropriate tests that are necessary on that component. There certainly is nothing wrong with using both approaches for one job. It will allow an instant check on whether or not you have done what was required.

## Start-up Day Procedure

Figure 20 has been drawn up to represent a more or less typical industrial system. As you can see, it includes a standby pump, cushioned cylinders, speed control valves, crossover relief valves, a sequence valve, a counterbalance valve, manual and solenoid-actuated directional control valves, and pressure relief valves.

Let us make two assumptions. Let us assume that we have followed the eight steps of pre-start-up work, and that during this start up we have encountered no problems.

A most efficient start-up procedure is as follows.

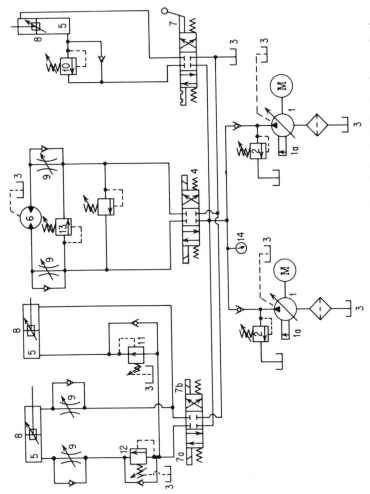

**Fig. 20** Typical multiactuator hydraulic system with manual and electrical directional control valves.

**Step 1: Lock Out the System Completely.** Lock out *all* electrical switches at the operator's station. Lock out *all* electrical switches in the motor control center. In doing this, you have total control of the entire system. It is not safe for you, your crew, or any other personnel if you cannot have complete control of the system. Complete lockout is the only safe procedure to follow. You will later be operating each directional control valve by means of the manual override, and therefore will not need the services of the operator. If an operator is needed, it is wise to make use of the personnel made available to you. Do not forget that in the section on safety, it was mentioned that you must instruct your people in regard to what is happening and what is supposed to happen.

**Step 2: Check for Safe Starting.** Make certain that it is safe to operate the system. Post your personnel in the appropriate areas to keep anyone from wandering into your area. Make certain that everyone knows the possible hazards.

**Step 3: "Bump" the Pump.** Unlock the pump switch. While you are out at the pump, have the electrician "bump" the pump again, just to make sure that it is turning in the correct direction. When you know that the pump is turning in the correct direction, have the electrician bump it three or four more times. The ON position should be maintained no more than a second or two each time. During this bumping, you should be listening to the pump to be sure that there are no strange noises. When you are satisfied that the pump sounds correct, that it is safe for the pump to continue running, have the electrician turn the pump on and let it run.

The pump, item 1 on Figure 20, is now on line and running. It is producing maximum flow. Most of the fluid is passing over the relief valve, item 2, to tank, item 3. Do not forget that previous to today's start-up, you had adjusted most of the pressure controls to the minimal position. In this case, the pump cannot compensate, and maximum flow is leaving the pump at minimal pressure. Now, turn the system pressure relief valve adjusting screw in to get about one-half of the desired system pressure as read on the pressure gauge, item 14. Now, set the compensator to about 100 psi less than the system pressure relief valve setting.

You will be able to hear the change of sound as the pump compensates. Listen to the pump now. Does it sound normal? Is it making an odd noise? In any event, it is appropriate to be ready to turn the pump off if it is making a strange noise.

**Step 4: Warn Mechanics of Actuator Motion.** At this point, hydraulic fluid is available to every directional control valve. If there are any two-position valves in the circuit, there may be motion of the actuator at this time, depending on the actuator's original position. In any event, your mechanics must be forewarned of this potential, so that they can stand clear of any actuator motion.

**Step 5: Run-in Pump.** Let the system run for about 5 minutes at this pressure setting. This run-in period will warm up the fluid and aid in eliminating some of the entrained air.

**Step 6: Bleed Air from System:** Working on a subcircuit basis, one actuator at a time, with no load on the actuators, have the mechanics just crack the hose fitting to one actuator. If the actuator is a motor, this is not necessary, since actuation of the directional control valve will allow the fluid to flow through the motor and back to the tank, carrying any entrained air with it. If the cylinders have air bleed valves, it is not necessary to crack the hose lines to get rid of the air.

**Step 7: Manually Override Directional Control Valve on One Side.** Manually override one side of the solenoid valve or manual valve for the appropriate cylinder or motor until some fluid comes out of the bleeder valve or hose. Release the override. Tighten the bleeder or hose fitting.

**Step 8: Engage Opposite Side of Valve Manually.** Manually override the opposite solenoid or manual valve until fluid comes from that bleeder or hose fitting. Release the manual override. Have the mechanic tighten the hose or bleeder valve fitting. You have now removed most of the air from that subcircuit. You must inform the mechanic of the potential of motion of the actuator when you override the directional control valve.

**Step 9: Check Actuator for Correct Motion.** Manually override the directional control valve in both directions a few times to check that the actuator is moving in the correct direction. This operation of the actuator in both directions will further aid in the removal of entrained air from the fluid.

**Step 10: Reset Cushion Valves.** Adjust the cushion valves to the desired degree. You must remember that this is not the final cushion valve setting. The final adjustment must be made with the cylinder loaded to the design load. It is a good idea at this time to set the cushion valve to a point about one half-turn tighter than necessary, since the design load will need more cushioning than the empty loaded cylinder.

**Step 11: Reset Speed Control Valves.** Adjust the speed control valve for the desired cylinder rod extension speed by means of the manual override of the directional control valve. Now you must adjust the desired cylinder retraction speed by means of the manual override of the directional control valve, and the appropriate flow control valve.

**Step 12: Reset Counterbalance Valve.** If there is a counterbalance valve in the circuit (item 10 in this case), the cylinder rod will not have been able to move when you manually operate the directional control valve, unless the setting of the valve is rather low. You had previously set it to its maximum pressure position. It is now an appropriate time to make preliminary adjustment to the valve. Place the design load on the cylinder which has the counterbalance valve in the circuit, and have one of the mechanics override the directional control valve to lift the load to the midpoint of rod extension. At this time the directional control valve should be centered, and the load will stay at that point, because the counterbalance valve is set to a point considerably in excess of the loading of the cylinder. With the directional control valve in neutral, slowly back off on the counterbalance valve adjustment screw until the loaded cylinder rod starts to retract. Stop turning the adjustment screw. At this point, you have adjusted the valve a little too low for the correct counterbalance effect. Turn the adjusting screw in one half-turn, and lock the valve in position. This is an approximate position, but it is functional for the time being. Fine tuning must be done later.

**Step 13: Reset Pressure-Reducing Valve.** If there is a pressure-reducing valve in the circuit, such as item 11, Figure 20, you have previously set it to its minimal point, thus preventing overpressurization downstream of it. It is correct at this time to reset it. To do this, you must now set the main pressure relief valve to its final setting, and also set the pressure compensator on the pump to its setting. In order to set the pressure compensator, you must first set the pressure relief valve to that pressure indicated on the drawing. The compensator adjustor must then be turned in until it is set correctly. Until this setting was made, there was but minimum pressure in the system. To set the pressure-reducing valve you need a pressure in excess of the desired reduced pressure. The system pressure relief valve is to protect the system in the event that the compensator were to malfunction in the uncompensated mode. The system pressure is about 200 psi higher than the design operating pressure to which the compensator would be set. Lock the main relief valve setting at the appropriate pressure and, then, lock the compensator at its correct pressure. For all the rest of the adjustments you will be making on this circuit and other subcircuits, you will now be working with full system pressure. You now have a functional system, so extreme care must be exercised for the balance of the settings.

**Step 14: Reset Sequence Valve.** If there is a sequence valve in the circuit, as item 12 in Figure 20, it is now appropriate to set it to the correct pressure as shown on the hydraulic line diagram. This valve had previously been set to its maximum point so that it would not open until you set it to the correct pressure point. Set it to this correct point and lock it.

**Step 15: Reset Crossover Relief Valves.** The crossover relief valves shown as item 13, Figure 20, should be set correctly at this time (about 200 psi over system pressure). The valve adjustments should be locked at the correct pressure point.

You have by now set all of the adjustable functions to their approximate or exact settings, and know that the various actuators function correctly when the directional control valves are manually overridden.

**Step 16: Have Electricians Make Their Tests.** At this point, you can turn the system over to the electrical people to run the entire system through its paces electrically. You have eliminated any possibility that there may be a hydraulic fault. Any faults which show up at the time of the various tests by the electrical people *must* be electrical in nature.

**Step 17: Make Minor Adjustments.** Your job of start up is completed except for some minor "tune-up" adjustments which may be necessary when the actuators are loaded to design loading. If, as in this case, there is a standby pump in the circuit, you must follow the necessary steps to set its pressure relief valve and the pump compensator, as in steps 1 to 5 above.

**Step 18: Readjust Main System Pressure Relief Valve If Required.** If, after having gone through all of these adjustments, you find that certain cylinder functions do not occur, you must remember that design criteria and machining capability are not infallible. You may find that some circuits will not function at design system pressure. Frictional resistance of new seals, tight metal-to-metal distances, and other considerations may require that the system pressure be elevated by 100 to 200 psi to give perfect system function. Make the necessary main system pressure adjustment, and any others that may help to put the system on line to accomplish the actuations that are required.

# 5

# SYSTEM CLEANING—
# WHY IS IT NEEDED?

To verify the need for cleaning or flushing a system, let us consider what can cause the need for good filtration and system cleaning. In an old system, and for that matter a new system, when the system pressure relief valve fails in the nonrelieving mode, system pressure will rapidly increase, since there is no place for the fluid from the positive displacement pump to go. As the pump continues to rotate, the fluid becomes more and more compressed until such time that the weakest part of the system must fail catastrophically to relieve the pressure. What will the weakest member be? It may be the coupling key or keys, pump shaft, piping, tubing, pump, hose, relief valve, etc. Whatever cannot stand the stress will be the first to fail.

Let us ask ourselves why we want to have a clean system. Our main goal is to have a hydraulic system which was designed to perform various work functions, at the desired design force and at the rated speed. We also want this system to be as trouble-free as is possible with a cost-effective design. In order to achieve these desires it is necessary that we perform those tasks that will lead to long, maintenance-free service life. The major cause of the need for maintenance on hydraulic systems is dirt in the system, which causes sticking of components and erosion of the internals of components. If you could eliminate, or at least minimize, these two items, you could expect your hydraulic system to go on forever. If you do not insist on and practice a good filter maintenance program, you must expect component failures. What type of component failure can you expect? The photographs shown in Figures 21 through 43 are examples of component failures which were caused by lack of a good filter maintenance program.

Probably the most detrimental failure, as far as the system is concerned, is the scrambling of the internals of the pump. When a pump starts to fail catastrophically, some parts of the debris are discharged into the discharge from the pump and out into the system. The particulate matter so generated will most certainly cause malfunctions of other components in the system unless the entire system is flushed and cleaned. The cost of the lost pump, the cost of the lost production, and the cost to clean

**Fig. 21**   Broken vane stuck in the rotor of a vane pump.

the system far overshadow the costs of the necessary filter elements which could have eliminated the failure to begin with.

### Vane Pump Failures

Figure 21 shows the edge of a broken vane which is stuck in the rotor. A poor filter maintenance program led to a buildup of particulate matter in the system. A particle or particles of dirt managed to get lodged between this particular vane and the area within which it slides. The particulate matter prevented the vane from moving inward, and the forces which were exerted were great enough to cause vane failure. As is quite visible in the picture, some of the particulate matter scored the rotor. In this instance, failure of the vane to move correctly led to failure of the pump shaft inside the housing.

Figure 22 shows another vane pump assembly. In this instance,

**Fig. 22** Damaged rotor with broken vanes stuck in damaged ring of vane pump. (Note points A and B.)

**Fig. 23**  Close-up of point A of Figure 22.

dirt caused one or more vanes to stick in their slots. The entire assembly is so jammed together that it is impossible to take the rotor out of the ring without some kind of press. When the vanes start to do some sticking in the vane slots at the point where they are supposed to be returning toward the centerline of rotation, and they do not move inwardly, they become cutting edges, and will cut into the ring until the force produced by the vanes following the cam ring is great enough to cause the vanes to move inward, or break off. The net result is a general, localized machining action on the cam ring by succeeding vanes. This situation is shown in Figure 22 at points A and B. When the notch in the cam ring is great enough in depth that the vanes are not pushed back into their slots, the force generated by the rotational effect can be great enough to cause failure of the vanes and the rotor, and sometimes the cam ring even fails.

Figure 23 shows a close-up of the groove at point A on Figure 22. Figure 24 shows a close-up of the groove at point B on Figure

**Fig. 24**  Close-up of point B of Figure 22.

22. It is quite obvious in both pictures that there is a definite groove in the ring. The abrasive effects of the particulate matter are also quite visible on the side of the rotor. The faces of the rotor and the edges of the vanes were grooved by the motion of the particulate matter being carried around the periphery of the port blocks by the vanes and the rotor. Figure 25 shows the port block for this particular pump. The circular lines were caused by this particulate matter cutting into the port block. These grooves are little flow paths for the fluid in the pump, and they will allow for interport flow of the fluid in the pump. This interport flow will give a reduction of efficiency in the pump, which may only show up in the case drain fluid volume, or in a reduced flow to the system. Needless to say, this system had to be flushed and cleaned before a replacement pump was installed.

Figure 26 shows a rotor with the shaft sheared off by the torsional effect of the motor driving the shaft and the resisting effect caused by the jamming of the pump interior parts. The entire spline has been distorted at a 45 degree angle, which is the normal angle of torsional failures. In addition to rotor, cam ring, and vane parts going out into the system piping, some of the fragments from the broken shaft went out into the system.

Figure 27 shows a close-up of the splined shaft of the pump. Notice that many of the spline fragments are missing. It is these small pieces of the spline that have gotten out into the system and will ultimately cause failures in other system components if they are not removed by flushing and cleaning of the entire system.

Figure 28 shows the surface of a broken-off piece of a rotor. The vertical lines on the piece were caused by dirt rubbing in the space between the vane and the portion of the rotor that makes the slot.

Figure 29 shows a rotor with a vane stuck in a slot. Notice the

**Fig. 25** Vane pump port block damaged by particulate matter.

**Fig. 26** Vane pump rotor with sheared shaft.

circular marks on the inner and outer surfaces. These grooves were caused by particulate matter being carried around in a circle at the junction of the rotor with the port plate.

Figure 30 shows a rotor which had failed catastrophically, but was reassembled for the photograph. The central core of the rotor continued to turn after the pump had failed catastrophically. Note the nicks in the outer periphery of various of the pieces. Figure 31 shows the central core of that rotor, which continued to turn until the motor was shut down. In continuing to turn, it had pieces knocked off that interfered with those parts of the rotor that stayed in the cam ring. Some of those parts had to get out into the system and caused other problems.

Figure 32 shows a close-up of one of the parts of the rotor which was broken off when the pump failed. The multitude of small parallel grooves cut into the face of the vane slot were caused by very small particulate matter being caught between the vane and the slot wall. The large gouges were caused by the catastrophic failure of the pump.

Figure 33 shows quite dramatically what happens to return line filters when the pump or hydraulic motor fails catastrophically and the material of failure gets to the filter element. The degradation parts are quite frequently pumped into the system even though a pressure filter is between the failed component

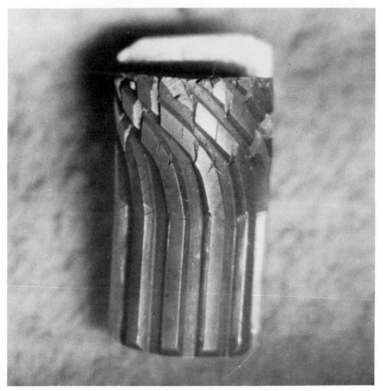

**Fig. 27**  Sheared vane pump rotor.

**Fig. 28**  Broken rotor portion of vane pump.

and the rest of the system. Filter element failure quite often occurs, and some of the debris gets out into the rest of the system.

Figure 33's filter was in a system where there was practically no filter maintenance program, and when the pump failed, so did the filter. Failure to keep a good schedule for changing filter elements led to a high particulate matter content in the fluid in the system, which in turn initiated the failure of the cam ring, vanes, port block, etc., until complete failure of the pump occurred. The filter cartridge was cleaned to show the effect of the particulate matter on the element. Unfortunately, the system was put into operation upon installation of a new pump. No cleaning or flushing operation was performed after this initial failure. The net result was that there were succeeding failures, which occurred with a reduction in operating time between each successive pump change, until such time that the cost of operation and delay times involved became prohibitive. Then, and only then, was the system completely flushed and a new filter change schedule begun. The cost of filter element replacement relative to the cost of hydraulic components and delays on the system is really negligible.

## Piston Pump Failures

The next seven figures show the results of poor fluid maintenance, and the effect that it has on radial piston pumps.

Figure 34 shows the rotating group of an axial piston pump that failed in service due to dirt in the system. Note especially the boss surrounding the hole in the middle of each shoe. Although the pump failed, these bosses are quite visible. Particulate

**Fig. 29**  Vane pump rotor with stuck vane.

**Fig. 30**  Reassembled grouping of fragments of fractured vane pump rotor.

matter caused a piston to stick momentarily in the bore, and a part of the shoe broke off. Note in the following figure, Figure 35, that there is no trace of any part of a boss on the shoes. This pump came from a system which had poor filter maintenance. The particulate matter in the system had to be there for quite a long time to abrade away the bosses on the shoes. As can be seen in the middle center of the photograph, one of the shoes is missing completely. Particulate matter caused the plunger of that group to stick in the bore of the cylinder barrel, and the shoe was pulled off by the further rotation of the pump. Because the shoe is swaged onto the plunger, and because it had worn considerably, it was pulled off the plunger. The debris generated by this failure caused further damage and ultimate pump failure.

**Fig. 31**  Fractured rotor hub of vane pump.

**Fig. 32**  Close-up of fractured vane pump rotor.

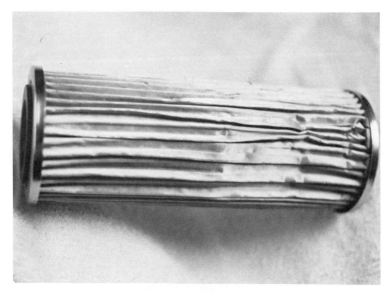

**Fig. 33**    Damaged element of pressure filter.

Figure 36 shows two plungers with the shoes still attached, but with portions of the shoes broken off.

Figure 37 shows a close-up of one of the shoes which was found inside the pump cavity upon disassembly. The broken-off pieces were not in the pump cavity, and must have gone out into the system.

Figure 38 shows a break in a shoe plate that came from a pump which had very poor filter maintenance. Notice the worn area on the shoe bosses and the gouges caused when the pump failed.

Figure 39 shows another shoe plate crack, and the extreme wear caused by the back side of the shoe rubbing against the shoe plate.

Figure 40 shows the wear plate upon which the shoes move. Note the gashes in the plate plus the peripheral grooves cut into it by debris which was caught between the shoes and the wear plate.

## Gear Pump Failures

The last three photographs of this series, Figures 41 through 43, were taken of parts of a gear pump which was in a system that had no filter in the system. Figure 41 shows the drive and driven gears of the pump. Notice the wear pattern on the face of the teeth. Dirt was caught between two mating teeth in the rubbing area, and initiated pump degradation, with ultimate gear tooth failure. The debris from this tooth failure initiated additional tooth failure. By the time that the pump had degraded to this condition, its output was negligible. Figure 42 shows the pump ring where the tooth peripheral seal was supposed to occur. A close-up of that ring, shown in Figure 43, shows the

**Fig. 34** Shoe assembly view of rotating group of axial piston pump's shoe plate with damaged shoes.

**Fig. 35**  Axial piston pump's rotating group, showing worn shoes.

marks left in the ring as the debris was carried around the ring, between the ring and the gear teeth. This created a large flow path between the inlet and outlet of the pump, with a great reduction in pump output being the natural result.

The Rexnord Hydraulic Components Division has a pamphlet *(Form No. S-121)* which identifies some causes of hydraulic component failures which you may find of interest. Your Racine vendor should be able to get you a copy.

Catastrophic failures of the types shown in the photographs must be expected if there is no filtration or if poor filter maintenance is practiced. Failures can also happen when systems use return line filters and the filters are allowed to go into the bypass mode for periods of time. The particulate matter will eventually be carried throughout the system. Suction filters of 149-micron size can hardly be expected to filter out particulate matter 40 to 100 microns in size, and if the particulate matter is ferrous in nature, it must be expected to either damage or jam some component in the circuit.

If, after pump failures of the types shown in the photographs, a new pump is installed in the circuit, without there being a complete system flushing, one must expect additional pump failures in a rather short period of time. Any additional pumps installed without system cleaning will ultimately lead to very short pump life. The dirt in the lines will ultimately get to every component in the system, and then it becomes a matter of an accident waiting for a place to happen. This particulate matter adversely affects all of the system components. Check valves leak, pilot-operated check vales leak, directional control valves' spools stick, solenoid coils burn out, etc. The list of failures attributable to

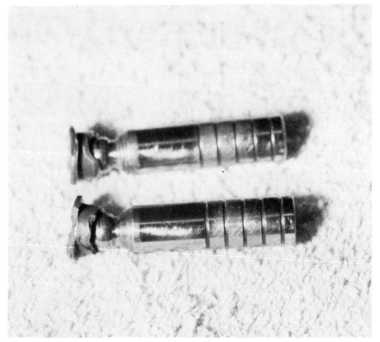

**Fig. 36**  Axial piston pump plungers with attached shoes.

**Fig. 37** Broken shoe from axial piston pump.

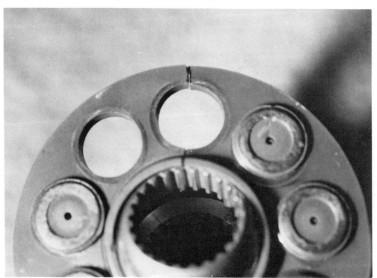

**Fig. 38** Close-up of fracture in shoe plate of axial piston pump.

**Fig. 39** Axial piston pump's shoe plate with crack and wear marks.

**Fig. 40** Axial piston pump's shoe wear plate showing abrasion marks from particulate matter.

**Fig. 41**  Damaged drive and driven gears of gear pump.

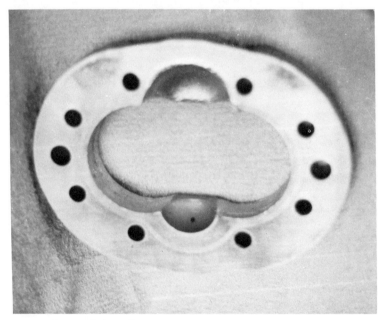

**Fig. 42**  Damaged ring of gear pump.

**Fig. 43** Close-up of ring shown in Figure 42.

this particulate matter is practically endless, and the cost of maintenance of the system will skyrocket, as will the amount of downtime required for troubleshooting and repairs.

The only way to prevent this from being a constantly recurring problem is to clean the system of catastrophically induced particulate matter immediately after the failure occurs. Refusal to follow the necessary procedures immediately will not eliminate the problem—it will compound the problem. The situation can only get worse, and it will prolong the flushing job, and increase the cost of doing the job when it is finally done. It always does get done ultimately, but unfortunately, a considerable expense for components and downtime has occurred.

With large-diameter pipes (over 1 inch) the flushing and cleaning costs are extremely high, but there is no inexpensive alternative. In the smaller-diameter pipe systems, the major cost is the delay time attributable to the cleaning process.

Let us say that one of these pump failures occurred to the pump shown in Figure 44. The system has no filter in use whatsoever. With the pump running at the time of failure, its degradation parts will naturally pass through the directional control

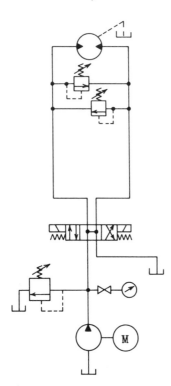

**Fig. 44**  Typical hydraulic motor circuit.

valve and on into the hydraulic motor. If the contaminants are large enough, they will ultimately cause catastrophic failure of the motor, and the pump and motor contaminants will get back to the reservoir. If a new pump and hydraulic motor are installed without first flushing and cleaning the system, it will be but a short time until the new pump or motor will fail, and thus introduce more particulate matter into the system. If component replacement is tried as a solution to the problem, the component life will get successively shorter until such time that someone in authority makes the decision to flush the system and clean the reservoir.

The wise thing to do at this time is to install an indicating-type filter in the suction line external to the reservoir and a filter in the return line, both sized at 3 to 5 times the pump's gallons-per-minute output rate, with a micron rating as determined by

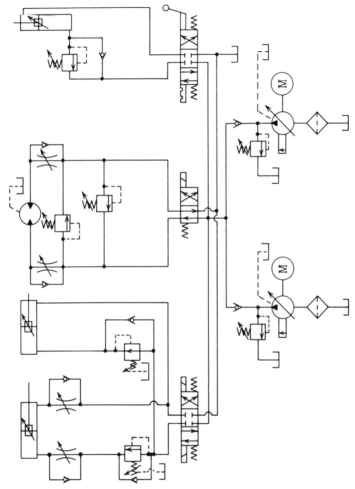

**Fig. 45** Complex hydraulic system circuit.

103

the pump or hydraulic motor manufacturer, whichever specifies the smaller micron rating. If the pump manufacturer calls for 40-micron rating, and the motor manufacturer calls for 25-micron rating, install the 25-micron filter, but make certain that it is at least 3 times the pump's gallons-per-minute rating. The suction line filter could be 75 to 149 microns at 5 times the pump's rating in gallons per minute.

If you have a system as shown in Figure 45, another set of operating conditions exists since the system is more complex than the system shown in Figure 44. Pump failure in the Figure 45 system will result in the potential for many more components to be affected by particulate matter, and can only result in subcircuit malfunctions. The spool valves can be affected by partial spool shifting, with the result that the solenoid coils will burn out, if they are alternating current coils. The check valves can be held partially off their seats, with leakage resulting and possible cylinder rod drifting occurring. The cushioned cylinders can lose part of their cushioning effect if the cushioning check valves are held off their seats by particulate matter. The pilot spools in the directional control valves can be short-shifted, resulting in slow actuator speeds. If there were any servo valves in the circuit, the magnetic particulate matter generated by pump failure would certainly migrate to the area of the torque motor's permanent magnets and possibly prevent motion, or cause motion to occur because the torque motor's armature could not get back to the neutral position. As you can see, the return line filter may prevent dirt from getting back to the reservoir, but if the filter were just at the point of needing to be changed, it would be bypassed with the extra dirt load and allow dirt to get into the reservoir.

# 6

# WAYS TO CLEAN SYSTEMS

The question naturally arises of how one should go about cleaning a system. Unfortunately, that is not the easiest question to answer, since it is a judgment call. The decision as to the approach to use depends upon the system design, the size of the system, the degree of cleanliness to be expected, and many other variables. If the system is a new one which has never even had fluid introduced into the reservoir, one method of cleaning is dictated. If the system is for servo valve use, another method must be used. If a small-diameter piping system with very few subcircuits is involved, still another approach to cleaning should be made. Past experience is the best teacher for determining the appropriate approach to use. If you lack this experience, you must rely on the experiences of others, and accept their recommendations until you gain the necessary experience.

## BASIC SYSTEM CLEANING REQUIREMENTS

In order to clean a system, and it does not matter whether it is a new system or an old system, it is necessary to clean the inside of the reservoir, the inside of the conduits, and the inside of the various hydraulic components which make up the system. Hopefully, the components that you receive from the factory are clean enough to be used in the system, so that leaves only two areas where in-the-field cleaning is necessary. If there is any doubt in your mind that the component that you are installing is clean, it is to your advantage to take it apart and clean it at the bench, and not out in the field. In most instances the cleanliness level in the field cannot approach that in a workshop.

This leaves us with the two field cleaning areas, namely the reservoir and the fluid conduits. Cleaning of the fluid conduits is normally called *flushing*, while cleaning of the reservoir is called *cleaning*.

## Important Cleaning Factors

In order to do a thorough and effective job of cleaning your system, it is necessary that certain guidelines be followed. These guidelines hold true for the fluid conduits and the reservoir.

**1. Fluid Compatibility.** The fluid which is used for cleaning the conduits and the reservoir must be compatible with system componentry, especially if you intend to flush through the various valves in the system. It is not preferred to do it that way, but on some systems and occasions it is necessary to get the system back on line as soon as possible. Under these conditions, running a jumper hose across the hydraulic motor or actuator, and flushing with an air-operated high-volume barrel pump, with the return line going into an empty barrel, may be the fastest approach. It is certainly not the most effective approach.

**2. Fluid Viscosity.** The viscosity of the fluid being used to flush the system should be as low as possible, to enhance the effect of the fluid on the particulate matter. You can imagine trying to clean a surface with a high-viscosity fluid.

**3. Fluid Velocity.** For highly efficient flushing, the velocity of the fluid through the system should be greater than the velocity created by the system pump. Fluid velocities in excess of 30 feet per second have proved most effective for all levels of system cleanliness. *Under no circumstances should you flush through a servo valve!*

**4. Reservoir Cleanliness.** The entire interior of the system reservoir should be cleaned with the appropriate cleaner using lint-free rags or cleaning materials. In most instances entrance into the reservoir is necessary in order to do a good job. Almost every reservoir that I have looked into has had some type of visible particulate matter in it, so I must impress you with the need for inspection of the reservoir. Any visible dirt must be greater than 40 microns in size; therefore, all visible dirt must be removed from the inside of the reservoir.

**5. Availability of Flushing Ports and Drains.** For the flushing operation to be absolutely successful, there must be adequate points for introduction of the cleaning fluid. There must also be adequately located drain points. The hydraulic components should be bypassed. The circulating fluid must be retained in a container for future cleaning and reuse. The bypass mechanisms, preferably, should be pipe or tubing, not hoses, since hoses can lose some interior particulate matter in the flushing process, and thus add to the particulate matter in the system. When the cleaning process has been completed, as a function of your having monitored the returning fluid and filters, it is suggested that the lines be blown out with oil-pumped nitrogen gas to remove the last traces of the cleaning fluid, if other than system fluid. As soon as possible after the blowing out of the lines, the system reservoir, which has already been cleaned out with the appropriate fluid and lint-free rags, should be filled with the correct hydraulic fluid, and the system started up as though it were a new system.

Admittedly, there are occasions when rebuilding of a component in location is possible—and necessary—and that is all that has to be done to get the system back on line. But, if a pump or motor fails, it is absolutely necessary that the system be shut down and cleaned. In either failure, the debris from the failure is likely to be transported throughout the entire system and induce failure of the other components in the system. This flushing and cleaning action is especially needed in any system where there is no pressure filtration between the pump and other components. It is also needed in those systems using one or more hydraulic motors without benefit of a return line filter. It is absolutely needed in those systems with suction line filters greater than 75-micron size. The debris generated generally includes particulate matter that is smaller than the filtration capability, and that material will pass through the filter and out into the system. Fortunately, the larger-sized material will settle out in the reservoir if adequately sized, but the smaller material may or may not be removed by the filter.

Experience has dictated that the system be flushed and the reservoir be cleaned before replacing pumps and motors which have failed catastrophically.

### Considerations for Flushing

The type of flushing to be used for a particular system should be determined by taking the following into consideration.

■ Can I go with a rapid flush until the next repair shift?

■ Will I be able to flush the system during the next repair shift, or will it be forgotten in favor of some other work?

■ Can I afford to spend the necessary time now in order to prevent an even greater time loss in the future?

■ Can my company afford the cost of replacing components damaged by this failure?

All of these questions must be answered before you can determine which flushing procedure to use on a particular system which has had catastrophic pump or motor failure. The various types of flushing procedures are listed below in the order of their effectiveness in cleaning the system, and simultaneously in the order of the expense of doing the job. The least costly and least effective procedure is item 1.

1. Quick cleaning using the system pump and bypassing the actuators only

2. Quick cleaning using an outside pump source and bypassing the system pump and actuators

3. Quick cleaning using mineral spirits from an outside pumping source and bypassing the system pump and actuators

4. Use of the system pump, bypassing all hydraulic components, and use of a transition piece on the directional control valves

5. Use of an outside pump source with mineral spirits, bypassing all hydraulic components, and use of a transition piece on all directional control valves

6. Same as item 5, but with use of system hydraulic fluid

7. Chemical cleaning, bypassing all hydraulic components, using outside pumping source, filtration, and appropriate chemical fluid

In every one of the cleaning procedures named above, the system reservoir must be cleaned by hand. The entire inside of the reservoir must be cleaned with a solvent, and then either dried with lint-free rags, air-dried with an air hose, or both. A fresh charge of clean hydraulic fluid must be added to the reservoir before the balance of the cleaning procedures are followed. New filter elements must be installed at all locations. None of the fluid drained from the reservoir should be used unless it has been filtered through a 10-micron filter.

The following figures show flushing approaches which have been successful. You may feel that a different approach is more appropriate for your systems.

Figure 46 shows a more or less average hydraulic system with three actuators and a hydraulic motor. As good installation practice would dictate, the actuators have hose connections for vibration isolation and ease of installation. Although there are filters in the suction and return lines, it would be advisable to flush the system if either the pump or the hydraulic motor failed catastrophically.

The quickest way to flush the system, if the hydraulic motor fails, is to connect the two motor hoses together and run the system pump for about 20 minutes, with the directional control valve for the motor circuit held in the actuated position. The return line filter should be changed before starting up the pump. This will provide a closed-loop filtration of only that area of piping which was definitely affected by the motor failure. In addition, the total pump volume is available to just one circuit,

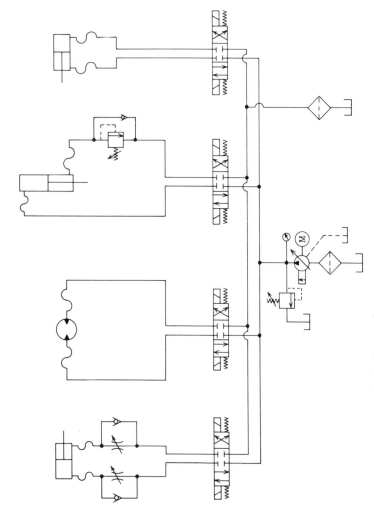

**Fig. 46** Multiactuator hydraulic circuit.

and therefore, the maximum fluid velocity will be sweeping the debris to the filter. Although this procedure will allow you to get the system back on line in a minimum of time, its total effectiveness leaves something to be desired, and it should be used only in an emergency. A new motor can be installed after the system has been flushed. A new filter should be installed at the same time.

If the pump in Figure 46 failed catastrophically, you could use a cleaning procedure with the lines hooked up as shown symbolically on Figure 47. Directional control valve transition pieces would have to be installed in all of the units, or a single transition piece could be moved from valve to valve. In any event, the maximum fluid velocity could be achieved by flushing one subcircuit at a time. In either procedure, the return line filter and the suction line filter must be changed before starting up the new pump. The reservoir should be drained and cleaned internally. Fresh-filtered, clean fluid should be added to the reservoir. In all probability the debris from the failed pump was in all of the pipelines, and some must have gotten back to the reservoir. The drained fluid can be salvaged by filtering it into clean drums through a 10-micron filter. By running the system for 20 minutes for each subcircuit, most of the debris will have been removed. All speed control valves will have to be opened wide before the flushing starts to ensure maximum flow rates. They must be reset after the cleaning process is completed. Although not shown on the drawing as such, the case drain line must be flushed also.

I must repeat that this particular type of flushing procedure is *not* the best approach to use, but it will get you back on line with a minimum amount of downtime and some assurance of security. Do not use it unless there is no alternative. A simple replacement of the failed component is not even to be considered.

At the very next repair shift, go through a thorough system flushing as shown in any of the other system cleaning procedures which follow.

The flushing method shown in Figure 49 or Figure 50 is much preferred, especially when using a flushing fluid of low viscosity such as mineral spirits.

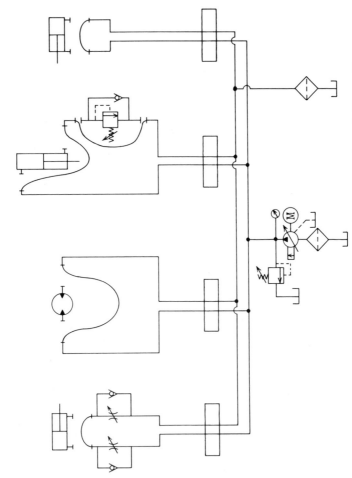

**Fig. 47** Hose and transition pieces required for cleaning system shown in Figure 46.

Figure 47 shows the system with the transition pieces in location. These transition pieces, or adaptor plates, are designed so as to make flow paths from the P port to the A port of the directional control valve and from the B port to the T port of the directional control valve. Notice that each of the major components is bypassed by interconnecting hoses, and the flow control valves are opened to their maximum position. This approach to cleaning is most functional when the system is allowed to run overnight, which gives about 8 hours to the flushing process. A new filter must be installed before the flushing is started, and again at the end of the process.

If you cannot take the time to flush overnight, the next quickest approach is to flush each subcircuit, one at a time with the adaptor plate in location. The other directional control valves will remain in the unshifted position, so that all of the pump's output will go through the circuit with the adaptor plate in it. This approach ensures that the total pump flow will go through the particular subcircuit. Removal of the system pressure relief valve for bench cleaning is to be preferred to flushing through the unit, since the bench flushing will prevent any of the dirt from getting into the reservoir.

If you have a system as shown in Figure 48, the procedure as explained for Figure 47 can be followed, but by making use of both system pumps instead of only one pump. In effect you are using the system fluid, but you are doubling the fluid velocities through the system. Again, the flow control valves must be opened to their fully open position. An adaptor plate can be placed in each circuit, or one adaptor plate can be used sequentially on each subcircuit as the previous subcircuit was flushed. Again, as in Figure 47, the reservoir must be cleaned and a new charge of clean fluid introduced into the reservoir before the two pumps are started up. New filters should be installed before the flushing and immediately after the flushing is completed. The fluid removed from the reservoir can be filtered through a 10-micron filter and reused later.

Figure 49 shows another approach to flushing a system. In this arrangement, an externally driven hydraulic pump of greater capacity than the system pump is employed to get the system flushed. Again, the system reservoir must be cleaned and a new

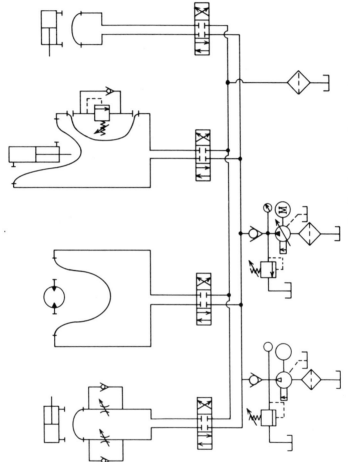

**Fig. 48** Using both system pumps to flush through valves but around actuators.

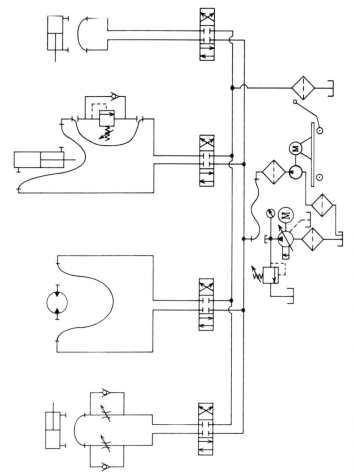

**Fig. 49** Using an external pump for system flushing.

charge of clean fluid introduced into the system reservoir. This external pump can be sized to clean all circuits simultaneously, and thereby reduce the time for the flushing operation. The filter cartridge should be removed from the return line filter of the system, unless it is capable of carrying the full output of the flushing pump. The off-board flushing pump can take its suction from the system reservoir as shown, or it can have its own fluid supply reservoir, in which case the fluid should return to the reservoir of the flushing pump. By using an adaptor plate at each of the directional control valves, you have assurance that none of the debris is going to adversely affect the directional control valves.

An additional side stream filtration system making use of a 5- or 10-micron filter could well be employed at the same time that the main system was being flushed. By using the side stream filtration simultaneously with the main system flushing cart, it is possible to get extremely good levels of cleanliness of the system, and get the system back on line in a shift or less. In any event, after the flushing is completed, all components must be returned to their locations and settings. New filters should be installed in the appropriate locations.

Figure 50 shows another approach which has been found to be quite successful, especially on pipes under $1^{1}/_{4}$ inches. By using mineral spirits as the flushing medium, in conjunction with an air-operated barrel pump, and flushing one circuit at a time with the adaptor plate, each subcircuit can be flushed in about 10 minutes. The return line filter to the barrel is 10 microns. When the first barrel of fluid is emptied, it becomes the drain reservoir for the second full barrel of fluid. In each instance, the fluid flowing into the empty barrel is cleaner than new fluid because of the use of the 10-micron filter. Depending on the extent of the subcircuit, one barrel of fluid is usually enough to flush the subcircuit. Before the barrel pump is turned on, it is necessary to get the existing fluid out of the piping system. This is best done by attaching an air hose to the point where the barrel pump would be connected, and blowing this oil back to the system reservoir before you clean out the reservoir. Any oil remaining in the pipes will mix with the mineral spirits, but generally is so minimal in amount that it will do no harm in the flushing process.

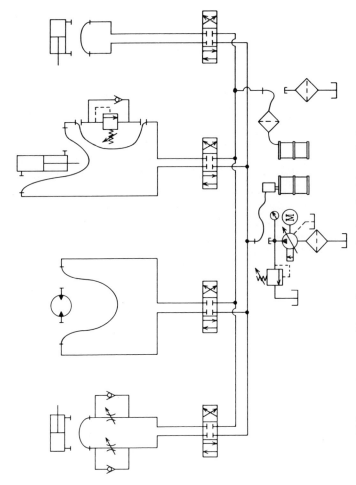

**Fig. 50** Using an air-powered barrel pump and mineral spirits to flush a system.

If extreme cleanliness is desired, by using one adaptor plate and a 3- to 5-micron filter it is possible to clean the system with one drum of fluid per circuit.

Chemical cleaning and flushing of a system is undoubtedly the one approach which will give the best level of cleanliness, but it should be done by firms specializing in the operation. All components would be bypassed with piping instead of hose, and the fluid velocities would in all probability exceed 30 feet per second. Since this operation is a specialty, it pays to consult the cleaning contractors in advance of the need for the job, so that you can have the necessary equipment on hand for them to do their job. They will need the appropriate electrical power source for their equipment, in addition to water and steam. In addition you will have to supply the necessary entrance and exits from your system. You may even be obligated to get rid of their expended cleaning solution after the job is completed.

Chemical cleaning is, by far, the best cleaning procedure to use, but it also entails more financial outlay and time to get the procedure accomplished. The degree of cleanliness is limited only by the size of your pocketbook.

# 7

# FILTRATION AND FLUIDS

As you have seen in the section on old systems and the section on new systems, dirt in a hydraulic system can lead to all kinds of problems.

Personal experiences have shown that those systems which have had good filter maintenance as a part of a good preventive maintenance program always have a history of very good component life. It cannot be stressed too much that a good filtration maintenance program is necessary. The major cause of hydraulic system malfunction is dirt in the system. In order to be assured of having a clean system, it is necessary that the fluid be clean as received, clean as introduced into the reservoir, and clean when it is pumped into the circuit.

You may ask, "How clean is clean?" The presence of *any* visible dirt in a system means that the system is not clean. In order for this dirt to be visible it would have to be 40 microns or larger, since that is the smallest size particle which can be seen by the unaided eye. What is a micron? By definition, a micron is one-millionth of a meter. Since 1 meter is 39.4 inches, 1 micron, therefore, is 39.4 divided by 1 million, or 0.0000394 inch. It has been proved that the smallest particulate matter that can be seen by the unaided eye is 40 microns, which is about sixteen ten-thousandths of an inch, or 0.0016 inch.

Since most of the clearances in the various components used in hydraulic systems are less than 0.0015 inch, it is not uncommon for "unseen dirt" to cause hydraulic malfunctions.

## SOURCES OF DIRT

Let us consider the six ways that dirt can enter our hydraulic system.

### Construction Dirt

Dirt can get into the system in the form of particulate matter which is the natural result of manufacturing of the various components which make up the system. The drilling and tapping of the various components results in dirt being in the various passages within the components. This dirt is not always removed by the manufacturers, regardless of their attempts at cleanliness. The various components are as clean as is dictated by the use of the component, but between the time that the part leaves the factory and the time that the part is ready for installation in your system, it is bound to pick up some dirt unless you are in complete control of the transportation and storage of the component. Dirt can and does exist in the inside of the pipes and the reservoir, which is the natural result of fabrication. Although great efforts are taken by the manufacturers to keep their finished products clean, there generally are some small particles of invisible scale adhering to the inside of the pipe and on the surfaces of the metals used in fabricating the reservoir. It just cannot be helped. What can be helped, though, is the dirt that is introduced into the system during its installation. The ends of all pipes which are going to be used in the fabrication of the system should be sealed, and kept sealed, until that pipe, hose, or tubing is ready for installation. All ports in the reservoir should be sealed, and kept sealed, until such time that the appropriate pipe, tubing, or hose is fitted into the opening. At that time, the seal on the conduit and the seal in the reservoir should be removed, and the hookup completed. A construction site is not a clean site, and unsealed items will pick up dirt. Some of the dirt that I have seen in reservoirs most certainly should not have been there. There is no excuse for finding welding rods, blueprints, rags, cigarette butts, soda cans, or bottles in a reservoir or conduit. Active inspection of the system is required to assure oneself that the system is being kept clean during construction. How can this miscellaneous matter be removed from the system? You must inspect the reservoir and clean it before you introduce clean filtered fluid into it. Once you have cleaned and flushed the system, you can keep it clean by maintaining a good filter changing practice.

### Container Dirt

Clean fluid as received in the barrel or by bulk delivery is not nearly as clean as one would expect. Although a high degree of precaution is taken by the supplier of the hydraulic fluids, for all intents and purposes, your fluid in the "as received" condition is not nearly as clean as you want it to be. Most, if not all, fluid suppliers filter the product before filling the tank truck or barrel. Unfortunately, these barrels and tank trucks are not as clean as the user would like to have them. This delivered fluid cannot help but have some particulate matter in it. The most extreme care in barrel handling and bulk fluid handling cannot prevent some visible particulate matter from being in the fluid. This "dirt" must be removed from the fluid by fine filtration before the fluid is introduced into the reservoir. It is very good practice to filter all fluid to a 10- or 20-micron level when it is being added to the reservoir. If you can arrange to have a system "fill" filter as the only entrance point into the reservoir, you can go a long way toward having a clean supply of fluid in your system.

### Breather Dirt

Once a system is on line and operating, the largest source of dirt that can enter the system is through the air breather for the reservoir. Unless the circuit design is such that there is never any change of fluid level in the reservoir, as in a system which has as its only actuator one hydraulic motor, every time that an actuator moves, there is a corresponding change in the level of the fluid in the reservoir. During this change of fluid level, known as *reservoir breathing*, air is either entering or leaving the reservoir. This does not occur, naturally, in pressurized reservoirs. But, in unpressurized reservoirs, each time that air enters the reservoir to replace fluid which has gone out to an actuator, there is an opportunity for any fine particulate matter to move along with this air and be carried into the reservoir. In order to stop this particulate matter from causing problems in your system it is necessary to have air breathers to allow for this air flow, but these air breathers should have a filtration capacity of 3 to 10 microns. The air filters must be large enough to prevent there being a vacuum or pressure in the reservoir due to system operation.

## Pull-in Dirt

Cylinders operating in dirty conditions have a tendency to pull some of that dirt into the cylinder each time that the cylinder rod is retracted. Although the rod scraper and seal may prevent most of this particulate matter from entering the cylinder, some of this particulate matter will get into the cylinder. The particulate matter will eventually migrate back to the reservoir and contaminate the reservoir fluid unless an adequate return line filter is employed. The use of rod boots and rod scrapers will minimize the amount of dirt that will eventually be engorged, but that is not the final solution to the problem. Return line filters will materially reduce the amount of this source of particulate matter.

## Maintenance Dirt

Each time that a component is removed from the circuit, or repaired in place, there is an opportunity for dirt to enter the system. When either of these two actions takes place, it is necessary to take precautions which will minimize the possibility of contaminant entry into the system. If a component is going to be removed from the circuit, it is necessary to clean off the conduits which enter the component, and also to clean off the component. The conduit endings should be sealed to prevent entry of any dirt. The component entry ports should also be sealed, if bench repair is to be done. The replacement component should be bench-flushed and air-dried, and then sealed until actual installation occurs. When a component is going to be repaired in place, the same precautions should be taken to prevent the entry of dirt into the system. It is a good practice to bleed the conduits to remove any particulate matter adhering to the interior of the fittings before the conduits are attached to the components. In addition to these precautions, it is an extremely good idea to provide good return line filtration.

### Generated Dirt

Generated dirt is the particulate matter that is produced by the rubbing together of two surfaces. This occurs every time that some part of the system is moved relative to some other part of the system. The generation of this dirt is greatest at start-up of the system, as the various components "wear in." Actually they are wearing out, but this major wear occurs early in the system's life. If this, and any other type of particulate matter, is not removed by adequate filtration, the hydraulic fluid will consist of a slurry of hydraulic fluid and fine particulate matter, which just happens to be abrasive. This generated dirt can be removed by a return line filter of adequate micron capacity.

## WAYS TO REMOVE DIRT

If long component life is to be expected of the hydraulic system, it is imperative that the particulate matter be removed from the hydraulic fluid by a cost-effective filtration system. The degree of cleanliness required for the fluid of the hydraulic system is a function of the system's sophistication and the degree of trouble-free service life that is dictated by the use of the system.

### Maintain Filtration System

The required degree of dependability is the determinant of just how much filtration is required. The dependability of hydraulic systems for commercial air flights is considerably different from that expected of a hydraulic press. Hydraulic failure of the airplane cannot be tolerated, while the failure of the press can be tolerated. The greater the degree of dependability desired, the greater will be the number of filters in the system, and the smaller the micron rating of those filters.

In industrial hydraulic systems you can use a suction line filter, plus a return line filter, plus side-stream filtration, and even use a centrifuge in addition to all the other filters.

Even with good filtration practices there can be some problems which may plague you. The adhesive used to join the ends of certain filter elements must be compatible with the hydraulic fluid. The O-rings must be compatible with the hydraulic fluid, and they must be of the correct hardness for the pressures involved. If magnets are a part of the filter package, they must not cause filter element failures because of their location in the cannister. Torn, damaged, or missing filter elements are other problems to be dealt with. And, finally, if electrical filter condition-indicating equipment is used, the electrical aspects of the indicator do no good if someone cuts the wires.

### Troubleshooting the Hydraulic Fluid

What types of filtration systems do you have in your various hydraulic systems? Are they doing a good job? If you have a great number of hydraulic component problems, the answer must be no.

What can you do about this situation? Answer: Troubleshoot the hydraulic fluid.

A question which comes up immediately is: How do you troubleshoot fluids? Actually it is quite possible, and rather easy, and possibly a new train of thought for you. Hydraulic fluid condition is an indication of the system condition regardless of the system and the fluid used. A look into the reservoir will, many times, tell you things which you cannot learn any other way. When asking for background information preparatory to troubleshooting a system, you can be the victim of the operator's memory lapses concerning past occurrences in the system. The fluid does not forget, and it cannot lie.

In hydraulics as well as surgery, "cleanliness is next to godliness." All too frequently, a well-designed system is turned from a trouble-free system into a constant headache due to the fact that inadequate attention is given to the changing of the filters on a scheduled basis, with the result that the filters go into the bypass mode. When this happens, fluid degradation and component failure must follow shortly.

If you make use of your senses of touch, smell, and sight, you are in a good position to make use of the facts that the hydraulic fluid can tell you. Open up the reservoir and look inside. Feel the fluid, smell it, look for bubbles or suspended matter. Look for a multiple-layer effect. Compare the fluid in the reservoir with new fluid. You should get acquainted with what new fluid looks like and smells like. Is the fluid in the reservoir the same color as the new fluid, or is it milky, darker than the new fluid, or foamy? Does it smell burned? Can you feel particulate matter in it? Can you see particulate matter? If the answer to any of these questions is yes, you have great potential of having some sort of trouble in the system. What could cause some of these conditions?

**Fluid Looks Milky or Foamy.** A milky coloration of the fluid can be caused by air bubbles or water emulsion. Where can water come from? The milky condition can be caused by water leaking in from a leaking heat exchanger, by water in replacement fluid, or by moisture in the air that is breathed into the reservoir. In most instances you cannot consider water to be a friend, and must expect it to cause system degradation due to its ability to initiate rusting of the various system components, and especially due to its lower viscosity.

Another cause of milky fluid is the entrapment of air in the system fluid. This can be caused by air being drawn into the system by means of leaks in the suction side of the pump, and/ or by fluid being returned to the reservoir above the normal reservoir fluid level. This return above fluid level condition causes the formation of bubbles of air as the return fluid traps air as it falls to the fluid. The bubbles may be large or small, and with a reservoir which is too small for the system, they may lead to foaming. Any foaming and air entrapment in the fluid will result in the air being carried to the intake pipe of the pump. Air in the pump will ultimately lead to cavitation, an increase in fluid temperature, a buildup of sludge and varnish in most system components, and overall system degradation. Look for the cause of the air entrapment and eliminate it if you want to have good system life.

The fastest way to find this air leakage source is to apply a thick grease at each suspected entry point in the suction line of the pump. If the air bubbles cease to occur, then you have found the leak source. Tighten the joint. If after individual testing of each of the joints, you still have an air leakage problem, turn off the pump and grease the pump shaft at the entry point of the shaft into the pump housing. Start up the pump again. If this approach does not locate the leak, you must check the filter O-ring seal for leakage. The O-ring may not have been replaced when the filter was last changed. A dab of grease around the seal area of the filter housing may clear up this leak point. Change the O-ring. One final point to check is the O-ring at the indicator shaft of the filter condition indicator. Change as required. It is possible, though, that the pump casing retaining bolts were not tight enough. Torque them correctly to the manufacturer's data sheet specifications.

**Fluid Smells Burned.** If the fluid smells burned, there are a few items which could cause this to happen. Those systems which require a heater in the wintertime do not need one in the summertime. Make certain that the thermostat is not stuck in the heat-on mode. It is best to pull the switch on the heater and lock it out for summer operations. Sometimes, the heaters are too large, in terms of watt density produced by the heater. This results in localized burning (overheating) of the fluid in the immediate area of the element. When this happens, the fluid smells burned, and it generally turns a dark color. Try to get a heating element which does not exceed about 5 to 7 watts per square inch of heating surface. It may be necessary to change the line voltage to accomplish this. In any event, it is very good practice to open the main switch about the first of May, and lock it in that position. You must not forget to turn it on in the latter part of September.

Another cause of fluid overheating is a leaking pressure relief valve in a system which has borderline reservoir capacity. If there is dirt on the pressure relief valve seat, there will be leakage, and heat generation. Worn compensated pumps and worn hydraulic motors are a frequent source of overheated fluid.

## FLUID ADDITIVES

Before listing some of the steps you must follow to ensure good component life, it is appropriate that you know some of the things that the petroleum fluid manufacturers add to their fluids to improve them. All of the additives may not be found in all of the fluids, but where it is possible and cost-effective to include these items in the additive package, it is done.

1. Viscosity index improvers lower the rate of change of viscosity with changes in temperature. These additives are particularly important in those areas where cold weather start-up can be a problem due to the high viscosity of the fluid that the cold produces. On the other hand, it makes it possible to economically operate systems where the ambient temperature gets too high for a nonadditive fluid. The additive allows for the best of both worlds by allowing for cold weather start-up and hot weather running conditions.

2. Antiwear and extreme-pressure additives are included in the additive packages of many manufacturers to reduce the rate of parts wear, and at the same time prevent galling and seizing of metal parts in the components.

3. Antioxidants are added to prevent fluid oxidation. When petroleum-base fluids oxidize, the products of this oxidation can combine with water in the fluid and form acids which will lead to corrosion of the bearings.

4. Detergents are added to the hydraulic fluids to keep the metals clean.

5. Dispersants are added to the fluids to keep sludge from forming by keeping the particles in suspension. It is the job of the filters to take this suspended matter out of the fluid.

6. Some manufacturers of hydraulic fluids add a dye to their fluid to give it a distinctive, readily recognizable color. The

color of the fluid also can be a great help in locating leakage sources.

7. Anticorrosives are added by some manufacturers in order to minimize bearing corrosion.

8. Rust preventives are added in order to prevent the rusting which can occur to ferrous metals of the hydraulic system.

9. Metal deactivators are added by some fluid suppliers to prevent the catalytic effect of metals on the oxidation process.

10. Demulsifiers are added to prevent moisture from emulsifying with the oil. As mentioned elsewhere, water can not be considered as being friendly to your system unless your system is specifically designed for a water-containing fluid. By preventing the formation of stable emulsions, the demulsifier will let the water drop out of the fluid, hopefully in the reservoir, if there is adequate residence time available for this to occur. This free water will settle to the bottom of the reservoir and be drained out periodically.

11. Pour point depressors are added to some manufacturers' hydraulic fluid to allow the fluid to be used at much lower temperatures than could possibly be done without the additive.

12. Foam inhibitors are added to prevent the formation of foam. If the foam cannot be prevented from forming, it will lead to pump cavitation and, in some instances, may even cause the foamed fluid to overflow the reservoir through the air breather. In certain instances this can lead to air breather malfunction, especially if the air breather is made of a material that is capable of being softened by the fluid.

13. Vapor-phase inhibitors are added to most ethylene glycol hydraulic fluids and to some petroleum-base fluids to prevent moisture in the fluid from causing rusting of the various components in the system, especially in those areas where rusting can occur, such as the top of the side walls and the roofs of reservoirs which may not have a protective coating on them.

If you are really interested in the chemistry of these additives, your hydraulic fluid supplier can give you all the answers you want.

## MAXIMIZING SYSTEM LIFE

If you are genuinely interested in minimizing your trouble-shooting needs, and maximizing your system life, the following list of items will go a long way to helping you, if you make use of them.

1. Keep your storage area for your hydraulic fluids clean and dry. This will help to reduce the potential of your adding dirt or water to your systems.

2. Keep the barrel bungs covered and sealed until you are ready to use the fluid. Clean the bung seals before removing them, and then clean the bung before removing it. Again, this keeps the dirt out of the system.

3. Use only clean pumps and conduits to transfer the fluid from the barrels to the reservoir, or from the delivery truck to the reservoir. Make certain that the entry port into the system is cleaned before you hook up the transfer equipment.

4. Filter all fluid introduced into the reservoir. *Do not use a bucket or similar transfer method.* Make certain that there is an adequately sized filter on the inlet of the fill port of the reservoir. A 10-micron filter will last for years if you keep your system clean so that frequent filling is not needed.

5. Make certain that there are enough filters adequately sized to give the system components adequate protection. Once these filters are a part of the system, institute and maintain a good filter changing procedure in order to keep the fluid clean.

6. If the reservoir is not pressurized, install an air breather with 10-micron capacity in order to keep out the ambient dirt.

7. Clean all components and conduits in the area where you will be repairing a component or replacing a component. Use only clean tools. If you must use rags, use the lint-free type. The premium you pay for lint-free rags will be returned to you in terms of longer component life.

8. If a pump or hydraulic motor fails catastrophically, drain the system, including the reservoir, and clean and flush as noted in Section 6.

9. *Never* add dirty fluid to a system. Trying to save the cost of a few gallons of hydraulic fluid by using dirty fluid will result

in extremely high system downtime and component replacement costs.

10. *Never* mix hydraulic fluids in your system without the prior approval of the manufacturers of *both* fluids, and even then it is not the best thing to do. It is highly possible that the additive package of the one fluid will not be compatible with the additive package of the other fluid, and you can end up with a fluid in which none of the additive packages can do the good for which they were intended. If at all possible stick with one vendor's product for a particular system.

11. If piping or component disassembly is required, make every effort to prevent dirt from entering the system at points of disassembly. Explain to the people who will be doing the work that extreme cleanliness is a necessity. In most instances, if they are aware of the need for the precautions to be used, they will exercise a greater degree of care than they would otherwise. If you make them aware of the fact that the average hydraulic system component clearances are less than those in the average Swiss watch, it may be just enough to have them exercise greater caution in their efforts to keep the parts clean.

12. If you must use tape to seal pipe joints, start the tape at the third thread from the end of the pipe. This will help to prevent the entry of any of the tape into the system as particulate matter, which could cause problems. An anaerobic sealer is much to be preferred over tape, since there cannot be any particulate matter to cause problems.

13. Never add fluid of the wrong viscosity to the reservoir. It can lead to system overheating if it's too high in viscosity, and it certainly will add to internal leakage of the various components in the system.

14. Do not mix fluid types in your reservoir. Phosphate esters do not mix with other fluids very well, and if they are erroneously introduced into a system which is not designed for them, serious problems can occur. Unless the seals in the original system are compatible with the phosphate ester fluid, they will be ruined, and a complete seal replacement program will be necessary. In addition, the entire system will have to be flushed and cleaned.

15. Make sure that all of the system components are compatible with the fluid that is to be used in the system. Take the

time necessary to check the manufacturers' catalogs to make certain that this compatibility exists. It is much easier to do this than it is to clean the system when the error is discovered.

16. Wherever and whenever possible, make use of cylinder rod boots to keep particulate matter out of the system.

17. *Make every cost-effective effort to keep the system clean. Institute and maintain a good filter changing practice.*

# 8

# ELECTRICAL CONTROL CIRCUITS AND SERVOS

As was said elsewhere in the book, of all the faults encountered in hydraulics, approximately 85 percent of them are electrically oriented. This rules out those systems which have manual pumps and manual directional control valves. There are more and more hydraulic systems coming on the market today in which most of the directional control valves are electrically actuated, and limit switches, relays, and control circuit logic have become an integral part of the system. When there are faults in these circuits, we end up with the 85 percent figure.

**Electrical Ladder Diagram.** Fortunately, the electrical "ladder" diagram is a very nice road map to show you what is supposed to be happening electrically to accomplish what is to be done hydraulically. When you see the ladder diagram you will understand the reason for the name. When you become conversant with it, you will find it a wonderful tool to augment your hydraulic knowledge. It can help you to reduce possible downtime by putting you in a position where there can be very little place for argument. You can converse with the electrical personnel in their language. You can manually override any of the directional control valves and show that operation occurs in the manner that it is supposed to occur. By using the electrical diagram you will be in a position to tell the electricians where to start their troubleshooting. As soon as they know that you are conversant with their drawings and equipment, there is a tendency for them to be less argumentative about the type of failure, and they get busy with their troubleshooting.

**Ladder Diagram Symbols.**    Fortunately there aren't that many different symbols involved for you to learn. Their electrical power must operate your solenoid valves. This is accomplished by the solenoid coils. In order to make your solenoid coils operate at the correct time—and only those solenoid coils which are to operate—there is a given path for the electricity to flow through. In double solenoid valves, especially in alternating current systems, you do not want to have power on both solenoid coils simultaneously; therefore there should be permissive and interlock items in the circuits to prevent this from happening. In addition, there must be certain controls available to take the power from the coil when the particular sequence has been completed. Preferably, limit switches or equivalent electrical control should be used. In addition, there are occasions when there is a need for a time differential to be available and, preferably, adjustable so that a particular sequence of events can occur in a definite time period and in a definite pattern.

Symbol no. 1 on Figure 51 is the electrical ladder diagram symbol which represents the coil of the particular solenoid valve that is to be actuated by the applied voltage. Symbol no. 2 represents a control relay, which is very much like the solenoid coil that is to be actuated, except that the control relay moves an armature which can open and/or close a mechanical contact, which results in the completion of or the elimination of an electrical flow path. The control relay has a fixed number of contacts which can be so oriented on the relay that any one set of contacts can be set in the normally closed position or the normally open position. Symbol no. 3 on Figure 51 shows the symbol for a limit switch in the normally open position. Symbol no. 4 shows the symbol for a normally closed limit switch. Symbol no. 5 shows two pushbutton symbols. The one on the left must be held in for current to flow through it. The one on the right must be

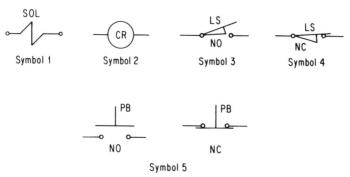

Symbol 1          Symbol 2          Symbol 3          Symbol 4

Symbol 5

**Fig. 51**  Basic electrical ladder diagram symbols.

held in to interrupt current flow. The left one is a normally open pushbutton, while the one on the right is a normally closed pushbutton. Both units are electrically isolated from the finger which would operate them.

Let us presume that we have a simple hydraulic circuit such as that shown in Figure 52. Operation of the no. 1 solenoid will cause the cylinder rod to extend. Operation of the no. 2 solenoid

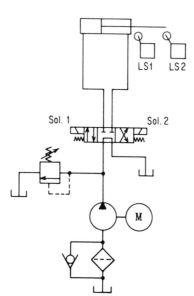

**Fig. 52**  Simple hydraulic circuit showing solenoids and limit switches.

will cause the cylinder rod to retract. Operation of neither so-lenoid will cause the cylinder rod to stop all motion.

If we connected a doorbell-type pushbutton of adequate volt-age and amperage rating to one of the solenoid coils, we could control that solenoid coil. As long as we held the pushbutton depressed, the contacts would be in a closed position and the directional control valve would remain shifted. If we released the pushbutton, the solenoid coil would lose power, and the directional control valve would shift to the neutral position due to the centering springs.

We could use a pushbutton to send power to a control relay which has various arrangements of contacts, which would permit flow paths or interrupt flow paths for the electrical current. The control relay shown schematically on Figure 53, left side, shows four sets of contacts which are controlled by that relay coil (side A). With no power on this relay's coil, the top set of contacts is normally closed and would allow current flowthrough if appro-priate wires were connected to the left and right sides of the contacts. The same holds true for the third set of contacts down. The second and fourth sets of contacts are normally open, and no flow path is available for current flow if the appropriate wires

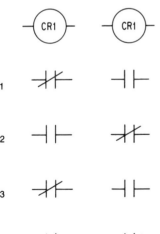

**Fig. 53**  Control relay symbols.

are connected to them. By supplying the correct amperage and voltage to the relay coil, *all* contacts would instantaneously be changed to the opposite mode, as shown on the right side (side B) of Figure 53.

If we now connected the pushbutton to the relay coil, we could use the appropriate contact sets to supply current to the solenoid coil and operate the directional control valve. Figure 54 shows such a circuit. By holding the pushbutton depressed, circuit relay (CR1) is energized and contact set CR1A changes from a normally open contact to a closed contact and allows current to flow and energize the solenoid coil, solenoid no. 1. This causes the directional control valve spool to shift position, which causes the cylinder rod to extend. As long as the pushbutton is depressed, the valve spool will remain in the fully shifted position. When the valve spool is in the fully shifted position, the rod will extend until it reaches the end of its travel, and stay in that position.

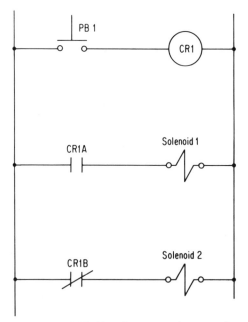

**Fig. 54**  Partial ladder diagram to show opertion of directional control valve solenoid coils.

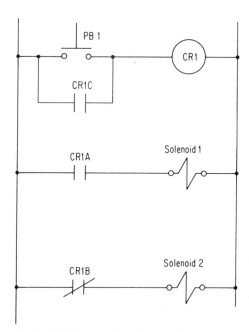

**Fig. 55**  Hold-in circuitry for pushbutton operation.

In order to be sure that no power is made available to solenoid no. 2, contact set CR1B (normally closed with no power on the coil for CR1) is instantaneously changed to the open position. As a result, it is impossible to actuate solenoid no. 1 and solenoid no. 2 at the same time; therefore neither of the coils of the solenoid will burn out due to dual loading of them.

Unfortunately we must hold the pushbutton depressed until the cylinder rod completes its travel. Fortunately there is a way around this problem. We can make a seal-in circuit which will hold the control relay, CR1, in the actuated mode, by taking an available set of contacts from the CR1 relay, which is normally open, around the pushbutton. When we depress the pushbutton, CR1 relay is actuated and, simultaneously, CR1C contact set closes and holds CR1 coil on line. CR1A causes solenoid no. 1 to shift the directional control valve spool, and CR1B contact points open to prevent solenoid no. 2 from being energized. Figure 55 shows this arrangement.

**Limit Switches.**  The arrangement shown in Figure 55 is all well and good, but there is now no way to take the power off the CR1 coil. We must insert into SOL-1 circuit something to show that the cylinder rod has completed its travel, and that something will simultaneously deenergize the SOL-1 coil. A set of contacts actuated by limit switch no. 2 relay could open when the actuator rod makes the limit switch move to a closed contacts position.

Figure 56 shows these contacts in the closed condition, ready for immediate opening when limit switch relay no. 2 gets power from the motion of the cylinder rod causing LSR-2 to close a set of contacts.

**Sample Ladder Diagram.**  Figure 57 shows the major portion of the circuit to cause the piston rod to extend when solenoid no. 1 is actuated, and make it travel to the limit switch and stop. Pushbutton no. 2 must be depressed to make the piston rod retract. As shown, the rod can go part way only if another set

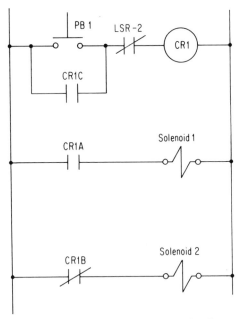

**Fig. 56**  Limit switch contact to open circuit.

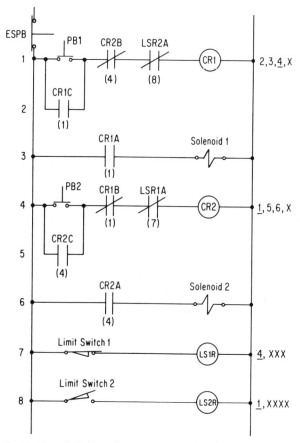

**Fig. 57**  Sample ladder diagram to extend and retract cylinder rod.

of contacts is inserted in the CR1 and CR2 circuits, which can be opened at will. Otherwise, full extension or retraction of the cylinder rod will occur. Installing an emergency pushbutton at the power supply point on the left side, as shown, will kill all power to both the pushbuttons. This killing of power will make the rod extension or retraction cease. Figure 57 shows that the rod is now controlled by the electrical equipment.

By now you can see why the electrical schematic diagram is called a ladder diagram. Each rung would appropriately be numbered on the left side and be given a line or rung number. The right side of each rung which has a control relay on it gets an identification of where the contacts for that relay are on the various rungs of the ladder diagram. A line under this designation indicates that it is normally closed with no power on the circuit (control relays in the deenergized mode). If there are any unused contact sets in the particular relay, they are designated by the letter X. If there is no line under the rung designation, that contact is normally open when the control relay is in the deenergized mode. In addition, each set of control relay contacts on a given rung is given a parenthetical designation referring back to the rung on which the control relay coil is situated. The electrical schematic diagram always shows elements in the NO POWER ON THE CIRCUIT mode.

**Time-Delay Relay.** To go into an automatic cycling of the cyclinder would require additional electrical control circuitry, which may include time-delay relays. Electrical time-delay relays can be pneumatically or electronically controlled. The delay time can go from milliseconds to minutes and be adjustable within the range of the timing relay. The timing relay can be of a type which has the delay time on energizing or deenergizing of the control relay. Each type of relay will have at least one set of contacts which will be affected by the timing device, and the set can be normally open or closed. There will be other contact sets which will operate simultaneously with the operation of the relay. The ladder diagram will indicate on the appropriate rung what type of time-delay relay is involved. "TDE" or "TDDE" will be noted near the relay. TDE means time delay on energizing the coil. TDDE means time delay on deenergizing the coil. There are special symbols for the contact set which is the time-delay set. The standard relay contact sets instantaneously change from their normal position to the opposite position when power is supplied to the relay coil. They simultaneously revert to their original condition when power is taken from the relay coil. The effect of energizing and deenergizing time relays is shown on Chart 1.

**Sequential Operation.** In some circuits, where there are more than just a few hydraulic actuators, the electrical ladder diagram

RELAY CONTACT CONDITIONS
TIME DELAY RELAYS

| Symbols | Status with No Power on the Coil | Status at Power on the Coil (Energizing) | Status at Power Being Removed (Deenergizing) |
|---|---|---|---|
| Timed Contact —o̸o— TDE | Normally open | Time out before closing | Instantaneous open |
| Instantaneous —\|\|— | Normally open | Instantaneous close | Instantaneous open |
| Instantaneous —\|/\|— | Normally closed | Instantaneous open | Instantaneous close |
| Timed Contact —o̸o— TDE | Normally closed | Time out before opening | Instantaneous close |
| Instantaneous —\|\|— | Normally open | Instantaneous close | Instantaneous open |
| Instantaneous —\|/\|— | Normally closed | Instantaneous open | Instantaneous close |
| Timed Contact —o̸o— TDDE | Normally open | Instantaneous close | Time out before opening |
| Instantaneous —\|\|— | Normally open | Instantaneous close | Instantaneous open |
| Instantaneous —\|/\|— | Normally closed | Instantaneous open | Instanstaneous close |
| Instantaneous —o̸o— | Normally closed | Instantaneous open | Time out before closing |
| Instantaneous —\|\|— | Normally open | Instantaneous close | Instantaneous open |
| Instantaneous —\|/\|— | Normally closed | Instantaneous open | Instantaneous close |

**Chart 1**   Time-delay relay contact conditions.

can be designed to perform a considerable number of sequential operations, by making use of a series of control relay contact sets which are permissive and/or interlocking in most cases. Every set of contacts must be closed in order for a particular solenoid valve to be operated.

Figure 58 shows such a string of contacts which you might find in automobile circuitry. The circuit is so designed that the following limit switches must be satisfied before turning of the ignition switch with the key will allow the starting motor to be actuated.

- All four doors must be closed.
- The seat belts must be fastened.
- The gearshift must be in neutral.
- The ignition switch key must be turned in the switch.

If any one or more of the necessary functions are not completed, the engine cannot be started.

As can be seen on Figure 58, there can be very complicated permissive circuitry available for permitting safe operation of equipment. If you are really interested in furthering your education in control circuitry, take the time to approach some

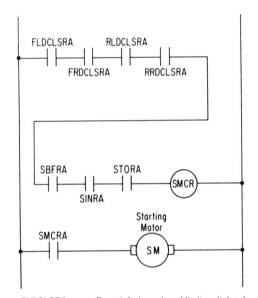

| FLDCLSRA | = | Front left door closed limit switch relay contact A. |
| FRDCLSRA | = | Front right door closed limit switch relay contact A. |
| RLDCLSRA | = | Rear left door closed limit switch relay contact A. |
| RRDCLSRA | = | Rear right door closed limit switch relay contact A. |
| SBFRA | = | Seat belt fastened relay contact A. |
| SINRA | = | Shift in neutral relay contact A. |
| STORA | = | Switch turned on relay contact A. |
| SMCR | = | Starter motor circuit relay. |
| SMCRA | = | Starter motor circuit relay contact A. |

**Fig. 58** Permissive circuit ladder diagram for starting an automobile engine.

electrical engineer in your company, and ask for further explanations. What you have received here is just the tip of the iceberg, but it is a good start. Pursue the matter further. I believe that you will find it will be much easier to learn than you think.

**Servos.** I would be at fault if I did not include a little bit on servos, since the future of hydraulics seems to lean quite a bit toward the use of servoactuated equipment.

The complexity of the subject is such that it cannot be covered here. You must attend one of the schools teaching the subject. There is some information which may be of assistance to you if you cannot attend one of these schools.

Experience has shown that when a signal is sent to a servo, and a response does not occur, there can be an electrical fault or a mechanical fault which causes this lack of response. An open wire or a short in the circuit can prevent the torque motor from receiving the signal; therefore no action can occur. There can be a mechanical fault if the bolts holding the LVDT are loose and the LVDT has moved from the zero location. There can also be a hydraulic fault caused by dirt preventing motion of the armature of the torque motor. This last item is one that can be corrected without too much trouble. Shut the system down. Drain the fluid from the torque motor housing, making sure that you maintain cleanliness in the immediate area of the torque motor housing. *Use only nonmagnetic tools for the job!* Use a hand-operated squirt oiler filled with mineral spirits to flush the torque motor armature. Your electricians can show you where it is. Keep the nozzle of the oiler at least 4 inches from the torque motor and flush it down with the fluid squirted from the oiler. Use lint-free rags to clean up the material that was flushed from the armature. You will find that this approach will solve about 50 percent of the torque motor problems. If this does not work, have the electricians replace the torque motor. Maintaining clean fluid is much more important in servo systems than in other systems, since the clearances in servo systems are so much smaller.

*Note:* Permission for the use of some symbols from the Joint Industry Council Electrical Standards, Item E 11.1 through 11.1.9 has been graciously granted by the Joint Industry Council of McLean, Virginia.

# 9

# SPECIFICATIONS

Now that you have learned about the considerable number of faults and problems which you can run into when troubleshooting hydraulic systems, it seems appropriate to give some thought as to what can possibly be done to ensure that a safe, efficient, and minimum maintenance hydraulic system can be yours.

Safety, a good service life, and system efficiency can be built into all of your hydraulic systems if you are willing to get involved in the initiation of hydraulic system specifications for your plant.

By having a good set of hydraulic specifications, you will not have to accept system designs which are inferior or inadequate. You can qualify to your vendors through your specifications, and in advance of the system design, those parameters which you find to be necessary. There are several advantages to this approach. Instead of having the vendors submitting a bid on their standard designs, you will have all of the vendors bidding on a basic design, which will make the process of selection, as a function of cost, much easier. The specifications will make it easier for your purchasing and engineering departments to make fair decisions on the purchases.

## KEY AREAS FOR SPECIFICATIONS

To mention a few areas where specifications will be of significant value to you is to get you started along the way to your own specifications.

**1. Reservoir Sizing.** Good hydraulic practice is to use a reservoir which is sized at 3 times the pump's gallon-per-minute output. If the pump output is 30 gallons per minute, the reservoir should be of 90 gallons capacity. Think of the advantages which can be had by having the reservoir sized even bigger, say a 4:1 or 5:1 or even larger capacity-to-output ratio. The price differential between the 3:1 and the larger ratio reservoirs is not too great when compared with the advantages to be derived from the larger reservoir. All the reasons for having a reservoir in the first place are enhanced by having it be big. The amount of dirt entering a system is a function of system design which will not change with the changing of the size of the reservoir. The amount of dirt per gallon, though, is a function of the size of the reservoir. The larger the reservoir is, the smaller will be the amount of contamination per gallon. It is therefore to your advantage to make the reservoir as large as is economically possible for the installation. The residence time of the fluid in the reservoir will be longer. The heat loss capability of the reservoir will be greater for a larger reservoir. The amount of air bubble entrapment will be reduced since the air has a longer time to escape from the fluid. The water dropout capability of the larger reservoir is certainly better than that of the smaller one. The particulate matter dropout of the larger reservoir is much better than what it would be for a smaller reservoir. When the cost differential for the larger reservoir is depreciated over the potential life of the reservoir, the cost per year to have this larger reservoir becomes very small. Probably the most important aspect of having this larger reservoir is the fact that the particulate matter per gallon is reduced; therefore the components in the system are exposed to fewer dirt particles, and the components therefore last longer before repairs are required.

**2. Filter Sizing.** Good hydraulic practice in filter sizing has also been a 3:1 ratio of the gallonage of the filter to the gallonage of the pump. Think what can happen by going to larger ratios than the 3:1 ratio. First, the frequency of element change will be considerably reduced. Second, the labor cost to change the element will be reduced. Third, component life will be greatly enhanced by having clean fluid to work with. Fourth, your element replacement costs will be reduced, since you will be using considerably fewer elements. Filters sized in the area of 5, 6, or 7 times the pump's gallonage will prove to be quite cost-effective. With the increase in component life, there will be a reduction in maintenance costs of the system, and a greater availability of operating time for the equipment that the hydraulic system is powering.

A combination of increasing reservoir size and filter size can result in reducing component failure to a bare minimum, and the cost to accomplish this is very low. In most instances, there is a substantial savings to be had by increasing these ratios. Over the life of the system, you can save many times the cost of going to a larger reservoir and using larger capacity filters.

**3. Conduit Sizing, Types, and Threading.** Your specifications can include a definition of conduit sizes and types, as well as threading on the ends of these conduits. This specification can materially reduce your leaks and, with the availability and costs of hydraulic fluids, can be a significant money saver.

**4. Safety Items.** Your specifications can include any safety ideas which you know are needed. All overrunning loads should make use of a pilot-operated check valve or a counterbalance valve. All accumulators should have bleed-off valves. Controls should not be located so as to be hazardous to the operator. Built-in working platforms should be a part of those designs which require maintenance personnel to work at high elevations.

## SYSTEM SAMPLES

The previous four items are but a few of the many items that could be covered by specifications. Let us look at a system that could be on a piece of equipment.

**Without Specifications.** Figure 59 shows such a system. Let us make a few assumptions. The cylinder no. 5 is a large-diameter cylinder to do some compressing, shearing, or stamping. Cylinder no. 6 is a clamping cylinder to hold the part that cylinder no. 5 is working on. The directional control valve no. 4 is to control the cylinders. As shown, there is no real control of which cylinder will work at which time relative to the other cylinder. There is no control of the speed of operation of either cylinder rod, and there is no positive sequencing involved. There is nothing to prevent either cylinder from shock loading at the end of the strokes in either direction.

**With Specifications.** Figure 60 represents what can be had by making use of specifications. Isn't this what we really wanted when we ordered the system? Without specifications, it is not what you will get. A suction filter with a bypass check is certainly to be desired. A system pressure relief valve on the discharge

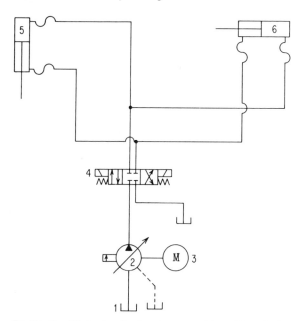

**Fig. 59**   Possible hydraulic circuit you would get if you had no specifications.

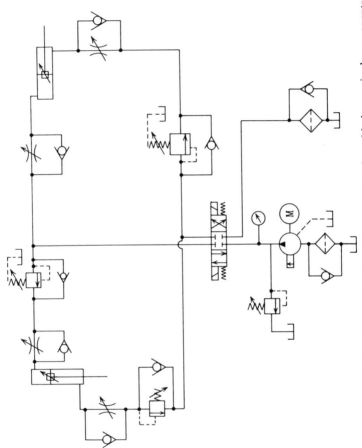

**Fig. 60** Same hydraulic system as that shown in Figure 59, but with the required components that good specifications could produce.

side of the compensated pump will certainly eliminate conduit failures if the compensator fails. The two sequence valves ensure that the clamping cylinder will clamp before the main cylinder rod extends downward, and the main cylinder rod will retract before the clamping cylinder unclamps. The counterbalance valve controls the weight of the larger cylinder rod to prevent free fall during any part of the work cycle. The speed control valves ensure control of cylinder rod actuation at the desired speeds. The cushion valves will considerably reduce shock at the ends of the rod strokes. Last but not least, the return line filter will help to keep the system fluid clean. Without the use of the specifications you could have ended up with the system shown in Figure 59. Which system would you like to have in your plant? As they have said on television, "You can pay me now, or pay me later." It is much less expensive to have plant hydraulic specifications so that you don't have to pay later.

# 10

# SUGGESTIONS

If you expect to be responsible for hydraulic troubleshooting for an extended length of time, it would be to your distinct advantage to keep records. Each time that you are called upon to troubleshoot a system, you should have two separate sorts of records on which to enter your experiences.

Keep a component card for each type of hydraulic component that you have had trouble with in the field. This record card would include such items as pumps, directional control valves, check valves, cushions, cylinders, and pressure relief valves. Enter the failure mode on the appropriate card. Each time that a different failure mode occurs to the component, enter it on the card. For instance:

DIRECTIONAL CONTROL VALVE:
1. Broken pilot spring
2. Stuck main spool
3. Spool plug loosened

The second component card should show the same title, but should also show the manufacturer and the valve designation nomenclature. The frequency of component failure will be pointed out to you by your own records. You may decide to redesign the system, or go to another manufacturer for the particular component. In any event you can use the records to show upper management that a higher-priced item is worth the cost difference. You can use the records to show upper management the possible need for additional educational assistance. Most important though, as far as you personally are concerned, the cards tell you what areas of what components can be the cause of problems.

Unless you have entirely too many hydraulic systems under your jurisdiction, it is an extremely good idea to make a file of each hydraulic system. Your file should indicate a complete listing of every component in that system, along with the appropriate component nomenclature as defined by the manufacturer. You should include critical pressure settings obtained at startup of the system. In addition, a complete record of the case drain flows should be recorded for each pump with a case drain, and each hydraulic motor that has a case drain. Samples of a Machine History Record Card and of Component History Record Cards with typical information filled in are shown on pages 152–155. Blank forms for your use, perforated for easy removal, follow the Index.

If you can manage to, make a separate history record card for each of these systems, defining system malfunctions and the steps you took to resolve the problems. Define the steps which you took which proved fruitful, and those that were of no value. Inevitably you will come up with your own troubleshooting techniqe which has proven successful to your systems.

Consistent success in troubleshooting hydraulic systems is a natural result of experience. Constant attention to the basics of hydraulics is necessary. Frequent referral to the following sources of information, in addition to your field experiences, will certainly prove beneficial to you.

**MACHINE HISTORY RECORD CARD**

Spark Wheel Machine
Location "A" Plant
Building _____ Unit Middle Bay
Hydraulic Schematic No. C1212
Column No. 18C

| Date | Malfunction Symptom | Assumed Fault | Actual Fault |
|---|---|---|---|
| 8-3-68 | Slow speed travel in north direction. | Motor O-ring. | Same (see CHRC29) |
| 8-22-69 | Head won't retract. | Bad cylinder seal. | Plug popped in solenoid spool. (see CHRC84) |
| 2-2-70 | Slow speed travel in north direction. | Worn motor. | High case drain. Motor worn. (see CHRC29) |
| 2-18-70 | Slow speed travel, both directions, south head. | Seal leaks in cylinder. | Speed controls maladjusted. (see CHRC91) |
| | | | |

## COMPONENT HISTORY RECORD CARD   Card Number  29

Component   Travel motor
Nomenclature   NFP-Y-RL

Manufacturer   "S" Comp.
Serial Number   27538
Used on   Spark Wheel Mach.

| Date | Remarks |
|---|---|
| 8-3-68 | A-port O-ring abraded away. Changed O-ring. |
| 2-2-70 | High case drain leakage rate. 9 qts per minute. Exceeds new case drain rate of 2 qts per minute. Changed motor. |
| 3-5-74 | New Serial Number  27889<br>Catastrophic failure of motor. Failed pump passed particulate matter into motor. System not cleaned after pump failure. |
| | New Serial Number  29947 |

## COMPONENT HISTORY RECORD CARD

Card Number <u>84</u>

Component <u>Solenoid valve</u>
Nomenclature <u>XYZL-QRTY-U-V-10</u>

Manufacturer <u>"Q" Company</u>
Serial Number <u>1234568</u>
Used on <u>Spark Wheel Machine</u>

| Date | Remarks |
|------|---------|
| 8-22-69 | End of spool popped out of spool preventing motion of cylinder. All P-port fluid bypassed to tank. Resoldered, and staked plug in spool. Returned to service. |
| 5-2-73 | Varnish on spool lands. Cleaned with mineral spirits. Crocus-clothed lands. Flushed spool. Air dried. Oiled and reinserted into valve body. Changed filters. |
| 6-1-74 | Spool clearance excessive. Interport leakage 100 cu. in. per min. Changed valve.  New Serial Number <u>1239987</u> |
| 4-4-75 | Solenoid coil at B-port burned out. Replaced coil. |

154

## COMPONENT HISTORY RECORD CARD

Card Number 91

Component  Speed Control Valve
Nomenclature  2U-E-3/4-72

Manufacturer  "Q" Company
Serial Number  None
Used on  Spark Wheel Machine

| Date | Remarks |
|---|---|
| 2-18-70 | Speed control maladjusted. Reset to design speed |
| 3-7-70 | Speed control maladjusted. Reset to design speed & safety wired. |
| | |
| | |

# SELECTED REFERENCES

1. Womack Educational Publications, *Industrial Fluid Power Texts 1, 2, 3, 4*, Dallas, Texas.

2. Parker-Hannifin Corporation, *Industrial Hydraulics Technology Bulletin # 0221-B1*, December 1976, Cleveland, Ohio.

3. Sperry-Vickers, *Industrial Hydraulics Manual Bulletin 934100-A*, September 1970, Troy, Michigan.

4. Sun Petroleum Products Co, *Sun Technical Bulletin B-4 A-930*, Rev. 9, June 1978.

5. American National Standards Institute, *Graphic Symbols for Fluid Power Diagrams, ANSI Y32.10*, 1967, reaffirmed 1979, New York, New York.

**TABLE 1 Cylinder-rod Extending Force as a Function of Cylinder Bore and System Pressure.**

| Cylinder Bore, in | Cap Side Area, in² | Cylinder Force—Rod-Extending Mode, psi | | | |
|---|---|---|---|---|---|
| | | 100 | 200 | 500 | 1000 |
| 1 | 0.785 | 79 | 157 | 394 | 785 |
| 1½ | 1.766 | 177 | 353 | 883 | 1,766 |
| 2 | 3.142 | 314 | 628 | 1,591 | 3,142 |
| 2½ | 4.909 | 491 | 982 | 2,455 | 4,909 |
| 3¼ | 8.296 | 830 | 1,659 | 4,148 | 8,296 |
| 5 | 19.635 | 1,964 | 3,927 | 9,818 | 19,605 |
| 6 | 28.274 | 2,827 | 5,655 | 14,137 | 28,274 |
| 8 | 50.265 | 5,026 | 10,053 | 25,133 | 50,265 |
| 10 | 78.540 | 7,854 | 15,708 | 39,270 | 78,540 |
| 12 | 113.097 | 11,310 | 22,619 | 56,549 | 113,097 |

## METRIC CONVERSIONS

| American Usage | Metric Equivalent | Conversion |
|---|---|---|
| Horsepower | Kilowatt | hp × 0.756 = kW |
| Square inch | Square centimeter | in² × 6.452 = cm² |
| Inch | Millimeter | in × 25.4 = mm |
| Saybolt Universal Seconds | Centistokes | Function of temperature |
| Feet per second | Meters per second | ft/sec × 0.305 = m/s |
| British thermal unit | Joule | Btu × 1055 = J |
| Gallons per minute | Liters per minute | gpm × 3.785 = L/m |
| Cycles per second | Hertz | |
| Degree Fahrenheit | Degree Celsius | $\dfrac{(F - 32)}{1.80} = C$ |

## Standard Graphic Symbols for Fluid Power Diagrams

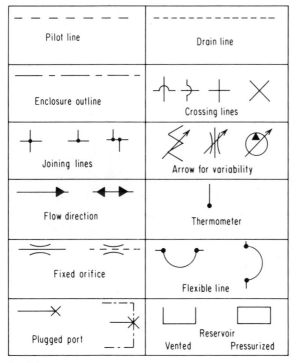

**Symbol 1**

Permission to use certain of the ANSI symbols from ANSI Y 32.10, standard graphic symbols for fluid power diagrams, was granted from the American Society of Mechanical Engineers of New York, N.Y.

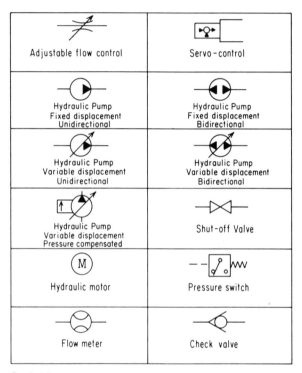

| | |
|---|---|
| Adjustable flow control | Servo-control |
| Hydraulic Pump Fixed displacement Unidirectional | Hydraulic Pump Fixed displacement Bidirectional |
| Hydraulic Pump Variable displacement Unidirectional | Hydraulic Pump Variable displacement Bidirectional |
| Hydraulic Pump Variable displacement Pressure compensated | Shut-off Valve |
| Hydraulic motor | Pressure switch |
| Flow meter | Check valve |

**Symbol 2**

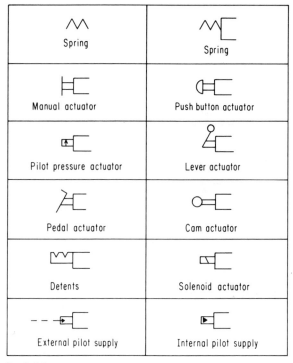

| | |
|---|---|
| Spring | Spring |
| Manual actuator | Push button actuator |
| Pilot pressure actuator | Lever actuator |
| Pedal actuator | Cam actuator |
| Detents | Solenoid actuator |
| External pilot supply | Internal pilot supply |

**Symbol 3**

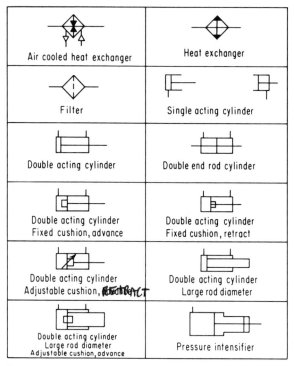

**Symbol 4**

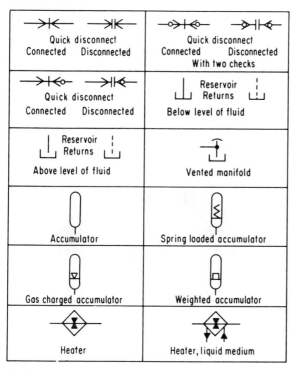

| | |
|---|---|
| ⟶>|<⟵  ⟶>|<⟵<br>**Quick disconnect**<br>Connected    Disconnected | ⟶o>|<o⟵  ⟶>|<⟵<br>**Quick disconnect**<br>Connected    Disconnected<br>With two checks |
| ⟶>|<o⟵  ⟶>|<⟵<br>**Quick disconnect**<br>Connected    Disconnected | Reservoir<br>Returns<br>**Below level of fluid** |
| Reservoir<br>Returns<br>**Above level of fluid** | **Vented manifold** |
| **Accumulator** | **Spring loaded accumulator** |
| **Gas charged accumulator** | **Weighted accumulator** |
| **Heater** | **Heater, liquid medium** |

**Symbol 5**

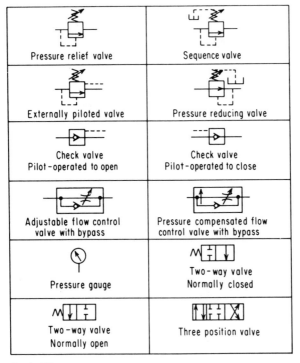

| | |
|---|---|
| Pressure relief valve | Sequence valve |
| Externally piloted valve | Pressure reducing valve |
| Check valve Pilot-operated to open | Check valve Pilot-operated to close |
| Adjustable flow control valve with bypass | Pressure compensated flow control valve with bypass |
| Pressure gauge | Two-way valve Normally closed |
| Two-way valve Normally open | Three position valve |

**Symbol 6**

# INDEX

## COMPONENT HISTORY RECORD CARD

Component _____ _____

Nomenclature _____ _____

**Card Number** _____

Manufacturer _____

Serial Number _____

Used on _____

| Date | Remarks |
|------|---------|
|      |         |
|      |         |
|      |         |
|      |         |

# MACHINE HISTORY RECORD CARD

| Location | Building | Unit | Hydraulic Schematic No. Column No. |
|---|---|---|---|
| | | | |
| | | | |
| | | | |
| | | | |
| | | | |
| | | | |

# COMPONENT HISTORY RECORD CARD

Card Number _____

Component _____
Nomenclature _____

Manufacturer _____
Serial Number _____
Used on _____

| Date | Remarks |
|------|---------|
|      |         |
|      |         |
|      |         |
|      |         |

# COMPONENT HISTORY RECORD CARD

Card Number _____

Component _____ _____
Nomenclature _____ _____

Manufacturer _____
Serial Number _____
Used on _____

| Date | Remarks |
|------|---------|
|      |         |
|      |         |
|      |         |
|      |         |

# MACHINE HISTORY RECORD CARD

| Location | Unit<br>Building | Hydraulic Schematic No.<br>Column No. |
|---|---|---|
|  |  |  |
|  |  |  |
|  |  |  |
|  |  |  |
|  |  |  |
|  |  |  |

# COMPONENT HISTORY RECORD CARD     Card Number ___

Component ___
Nomenclature ___

Manufacturer ___
Serial Number ___
Used on ___

| Date | Remarks |
|------|---------|
|      |         |
|      |         |
|      |         |
|      |         |

# COMPONENT HISTORY RECORD CARD

Card Number ___

Component ___
Nomenclature ___

Manufacturer ___
Serial Number ___
Used on ___

| Date | Remarks |
|------|---------|
|      |         |
|      |         |
|      |         |
|      |         |

# COMPONENT HISTORY RECORD CARD

Card Number __

Component _____
Nomenclature _____

Manufacturer _____
Serial Number _____
Used on _____

| Date | Remarks |
|------|---------|
|      |         |
|      |         |
|      |         |
|      |         |

## MACHINE HISTORY RECORD CARD

| Location | Building | Unit | Hydraulic Schematic No. Column No. |
|---|---|---|---|
| | | | |
| | | | |
| | | | |
| | | | |
| | | | |
| | | | |

# COMPONENT HISTORY RECORD CARD      Card Number ___

Component ___
Nomenclature ___

Manufacturer ___
Serial Number ___
Used on ___

| Date | Remarks |
|------|---------|
|      |         |
|      |         |
|      |         |
|      |         |

# COMPONENT HISTORY RECORD CARD

Card Number ___

Component ___
Nomenclature ___

Manufacturer ___
Serial Number ___
Used on ___

| Date | Remarks |
|------|---------|
|      |         |
|      |         |
|      |         |
|      |         |

# COMPONENT HISTORY RECORD CARD

Card Number ___

Component ___
Nomenclature ___

Manufacturer ___
Serial Number ___
Used on ___

| Date | Remarks |
|------|---------|
|      |         |
|      |         |
|      |         |
|      |         |

**MACHINE HISTORY RECORD CARD**

| Location | Unit | | Hydraulic Schematic No. |
|---|---|---|---|
| | Building | | Column No. |
| | | | |
| | | | |
| | | | |
| | | | |
| | | | |
| | | | |

# COMPONENT HISTORY RECORD CARD          Card Number ___

Component ___          Manufacturer ___
Nomenclature ___       Serial Number ___
                       Used on ___

| Date | Remarks |
|------|---------|
|      |         |
|      |         |
|      |         |
|      |         |

# COMPONENT HISTORY RECORD CARD

Card Number ___

Component ___
Nomenclature ___

Manufacturer ___
Serial Number ___
Used on ___

| Date | Remarks |
|------|---------|
|      |         |
|      |         |
|      |         |
|      |         |

# COMPONENT HISTORY RECORD CARD

Card Number ___

Component ___
Nomenclature ___

Manufacturer ___
Serial Number ___
Used on ___

| Date | Remarks |
|------|---------|
|      |         |
|      |         |
|      |         |
|      |         |

## MACHINE HISTORY RECORD CARD

| Location | Building | Unit | | Hydraulic Schematic No.<br>Column No. |
|---|---|---|---|---|
| | | | | |
| | | | | |
| | | | | |
| | | | | |
| | | | | |
| | | | | |

# COMPONENT HISTORY RECORD CARD    Card Number ___

Component ___
Nomenclature ___

Manufacturer ___
Serial Number ___
Used on ___

| Date | Remarks |
|------|---------|
|      |         |
|      |         |
|      |         |
|      |         |

# COMPONENT HISTORY RECORD CARD

Card Number ___

Component ___
Nomenclature ___

Manufacturer ___
Serial Number ___
Used on ___

| Date | Remarks |
|------|---------|
|      |         |
|      |         |
|      |         |
|      |         |

# COMPONENT HISTORY RECORD CARD

Card Number ___

Component ___
Nomenclature ___

Manufacturer ___
Serial Number ___
Used on ___

| Date | Remarks |
|------|---------|
|      |         |
|      |         |
|      |         |
|      |         |

## MACHINE HISTORY RECORD CARD

| Location | Building Unit | | Hydraulic Schematic No. Column No. |
|---|---|---|---|
| | | | |
| | | | |
| | | | |
| | | | |
| | | | |
| | | | |

# COMPONENT HISTORY RECORD CARD    Card Number ___

Component ___
Nomenclature ___

Manufacturer ___
Serial Number ___
Used on ___

| Date | Remarks |
|------|---------|
|      |         |
|      |         |
|      |         |
|      |         |

# COMPONENT HISTORY RECORD CARD

Card Number _____

Component _____
Nomenclature _____

Manufacturer _____
Serial Number _____
Used on _____

| Date | Remarks |
|------|---------|
|      |         |
|      |         |
|      |         |
|      |         |

# COMPONENT HISTORY RECORD CARD

Card Number ___

Component ___
Nomenclature ___

Manufacturer ___
Serial Number ___
Used on ___

| Date | Remarks |
|------|---------|
|      |         |
|      |         |
|      |         |
|      |         |

## MACHINE HISTORY RECORD CARD

| Location | Building | Unit | Hydraulic Schematic No. Column No. | | |
|---|---|---|---|---|---|
| | | | | | |
| | | | | | |
| | | | | | |
| | | | | | |
| | | | | | |
| | | | | | |

# COMPONENT HISTORY RECORD CARD    Card Number ___

Component ___
Nomenclature ___

Manufacturer ___
Serial Number ___
Used on ___

| Date | Remarks |
|------|---------|
|      |         |
|      |         |
|      |         |
|      |         |

# COMPONENT HISTORY RECORD CARD

Card Number _____

Manufacturer _____
Serial Number _____
Used on _____

Component _____
Nomenclature _____

| Date | Remarks |
|------|---------|
|      |         |
|      |         |
|      |         |
|      |         |

# COMPONENT HISTORY RECORD CARD

Component _____

Nomenclature _____

Manufacturer _____

Serial Number _____

Used on _____

Card Number _____

| Date | Remarks |
|------|---------|
|      |         |
|      |         |
|      |         |